1976

QUILTMAKING &
QUILTMAKERS

Quiltmaking

&Quiltmakers

MARILYN LITHGOW

PHOTOGRAPHS BY PETER KIAR

FUNK & WAGNALLS   NEW YORK

Designed by Ingrid Beckman

Manufactured in the United States of America

ISBN 0-308-10089-1

2 3 4 5 6 7 8 9 10

Library of Congress Cataloging in Publication Data

Lithgow, Marilyn.
    Quiltmaking & quiltmakers.

    1. Quilting. I. Title.
TT835.L57   1974   746.4'3   73-18042
ISBN 0-308-10089-1

Dedicated to my parents
Lorene Ulrich Wagner and
Ezra Christian Wagner

ACKNOWLEDGMENTS

A note of appreciation to Mrs. Mattie Bachman and Aunt Olive Fischer and to the quilters at the Maplelawn Home in Eureka, Illinois, and at the Mennonite Church in Meadows, Illinois, who shared with me their vast knowledge of quiltmaking and graciously permitted me to publish their photographs. And to the following people who contributed their quilts for this book: Frank Ackerman, Emma Bertsche, Alma Eyman, Olive Fischer, Alice Miller, Florence Mitchell, Viola Mundt, Reva Noe, Viola Rediger, Edna Rocke, Grace Rocke, Amelia Schrock, Martha Silliman, Myrtle Whitmar, and Celeste Zehr.

To my cousin, Ethel Reeser Cosco, goes the credit for most of the pioneer history of the Christian Reeser family, which she compiled some years ago from the recollections of Christian and Barbara Reeser's surviving children.

Without the encouragement of my family and friends—Kenneth Lithgow, Aunt Pearl Yoder, Dick and Judy Wagner, Caroline and Donald Sutphin, Susan and Giuliano Arcamone, John Hart, and Bunny and Peter Mudd—this book would never have been written. My heartfelt thanks to you all.

CONTENTS

A. "Golden Glow" pieced quilt made by my Great-Aunt Fanny Schrock.

B. *(above)* "Rose of Sharon" appliqué quilt made in 1852.

C. *(opposite page)* Details from: *(top left)* "Improved Nine-Patch" pieced quilt.
(top right) "Dresden Plate" pieced quilt.
(bottom left) "Flower Garden" pieced quilt.
(bottom right) "Tulip" appliqué quilt.

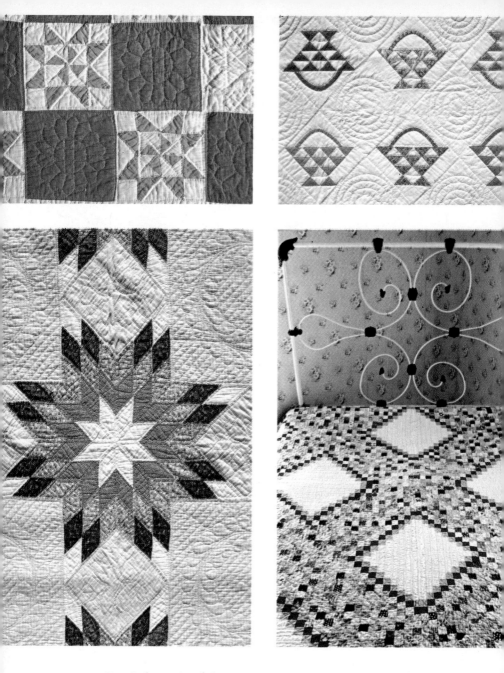

D. Details from: *(top left)* "Pieced Star" quilt.
(top right) "Basket" appliqué quilt.
(bottom left) "Star of Bethlehem" pieced quilt.
(bottom right) "Quilt of a Thousand Prints" pieced quilt.

E. *(above)* "Rose of Sharon" appliqué quilt of hand-dyed fabric.
(below) Detail from "Century" pieced quilt.

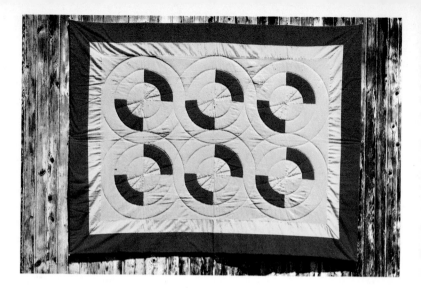

F. Contemporary quilts made by author: *(above)* "Geometry 101."
(below) "Glory Halleluiah!" and "Maneuvering with Difficulty"
(original designs by Susan Wilson Arcamone)..

G. *(left)* Aunt Olive Fischer with "Flower Garden" pieced quilt.
(below) "Rock Garden" pieced quilt.
(bottom) "Star of Hope" pieced quilt.

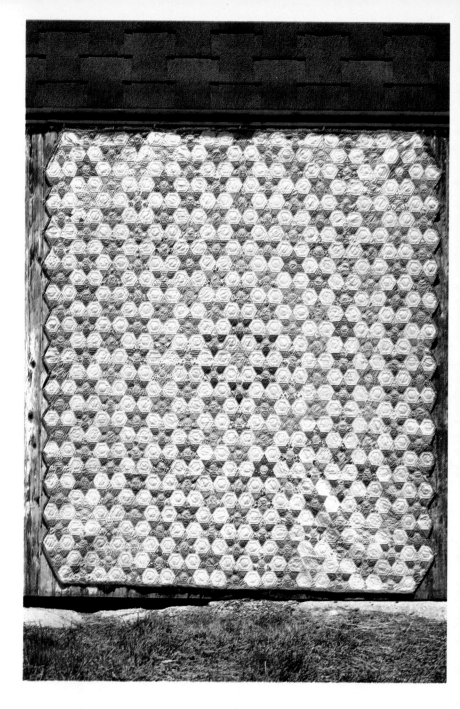

H. Six-point "Evening Star" pieced quilt made by Mrs. Martha Silliman.

QUILT PATTERNS
ILLUSTRATED

(For variant names, page numbers refer to text where name is mentioned.)

CHAPTER I
An Introduction to Quiltmaking

Quilting is an ancient craft that has been practiced throughout the world from China to Europe, but the patchwork quilts with their bold, vigorous designs are as authentically American as the banana split. I might never have experienced the satisfactions of quiltmaking if I had not lived abroad where, feeling isolated by the language barrier and lonesome for familiar associations, I decided to make a patchwork quilt like the ones I remembered from my childhood in central Illinois. By the time I finished that first quilt, I had become expert at ripping out stitches and beginning all over again to try to make the pieces fit together. And I had developed an acute backache from bending over the improvised quilting frame because it had not occurred to me that the quilt should be rolled on the frame so the middle portion could be easily worked on.

Since then I have learned that making a quilt is easy once you know how to go about it, and in this book I want to share with you some practical guidelines to the traditional techniques of quiltmaking as well as the results of my own trial-and-error experiments in making contemporary quilts. Also, I want to give you some glimpses into the lives of the midwestern farm women for whom quiltmaking is an enjoyable part of their daily lives. Not only do the Mennonite churchwomen, who are my kinfolk, continue to make quilts for their families as their grandmothers did before them, but they also hold quilting bees to fill custom quilting orders and donate quilts to annual fund-raising auctions for church projects.

Quilting is simply the process of joining together layers of materials by very short running stitches. As a practical means of providing extra warmth and protection, quilted fabrics have been used for centuries as clothing, padding for armor, curtains, and bed coverings. A quilted bed covering usually has three layers—the decorative top, the filler or "batting," and the plain backing. A "pieced" quilt top is made by stitching together pieces of cloth called "patches" that have been cut in geometric shapes to form a design. In "appliqué" quilts the design is formed by pieces cut from whole cloth that have been "laid on" a plain background and stitched down. The term "patchwork," as used in America, designates both pieced and appliqué quilts. A third type of quilt, the traditionally all-white quilt, has a plain top and the design is formed by elaborately patterned quilting, exquisite needlework that only experienced quilters accomplish.

The overall design of both the pieced and appliqué quilts is usually divided into "blocks" which repeat a pattern that forms a total design when the blocks are "set" together to make the finished top. The three layers of the quilt—the top, batting, and backing—then are "put in" a quilting frame to hold them taut and are stitched together in a pattern that is marked first in chalk or soft pencil on the top of the quilt. Sometimes, instead of being stitched through, the three layers are tied together with knots of yarn, and the resulting bed cover is called a "comforter" or "comfortable," as Christiana Holmes Tillson called it in her account of pioneer life on the frontier in southern Illinois during the early 1820s.

Mrs. Tillson came to the wilderness with her newly wedded husband from their native Massachusetts. The quilts and featherbeds that were part of her trousseau had been lost on the way and warm bed covers were urgently needed. Fortunately she had brought with her enough new cloth to make the top and backing for her comfortable, but the difficulty lay in preparing enough cotton to use as batting. She had to purchase twenty pounds of cotton in the seed, which, after it was hand-cleaned, yielded one-third cotton and two-thirds seeds, and ruined her fingernails in the process, as she noted in her memoirs.

Then she borrowed "kairds" or carding combs from her neighbors and spent a week carding the cotton and making it into batting. A quilting frame was made and set up, the layers of new cloth were filled with the batting and tied together, and finally "the great affair of making a comfortable" was completed.

Mrs. Tillson undoubtedly had made all the quilts and comforters for her trousseau, as girls were trained to sew when they were very young and were expected to have made a baker's dozen quilts by the time they married. Needlework was not a pleasant pastime but an economic necessity. Every piece of clothing and all household linens had to be stitched by hand, and only the very wealthy could afford to purchase the quilted bed coverings and curtains that provided a degree of comfort in the days before central heating. Quilts and bed hangings were included in the items listed in old wills as valuable property to be handed down to the next generation. It was not until well after the Civil War era that ready-made blankets came into general household use, and the necessity for making quilts and comforters at home began to wane.

The old pieced quilts with their bold designs that we admire today were born out of economic necessity too. New cloth was scarce and expensive in the early colonial days and later on the new frontiers as the pioneers moved westward, and what cloth was available usually had to be made into new clothing. The pioneer housewife had two choices in making her bed coverings—she could use the contents of her scrap bag, all the precious patches of cloth that she had saved from worn-out clothing, or she could make her own cloth from home-grown flax and wool as did the neighbors from whom Mrs. Tillson borrowed the carding combs. Preparing flax and wool into usable fibers that could be woven into linsey-woolsey and then dyed with indigo or other vegetable dyes was a lengthy, tedious process. However, the contents of the scrap bag provided a variety of colored and patterned cloth, and the quiltmaker, by attempting a design in her quilt top, could add a spot of color to her drab pioneer home. Neighbors traded patches of cloth back and forth and also helped each other finish their quilts at quilting bees, which provided a welcome opportunity for social gatherings.

On the other hand, the appliqué quilts made during the early colonial days were a symbol of affluence. While frugal New England housewives considered it wasteful to cut up new cloth to make an appliqué design when they had the bountiful contents of their scrap bags to use in making sturdy pieced quilts, the majority of the very old appliqué quilts were made in the South. The wives and daughters of the southern plantation owners engaged in fine needlework on delicate cottons, silks, and linens to make decorative counterpanes, and slaves made the bed coverings for everyday use. Another regional difference exhibited in very old quilts, and one that gives a clue to the approximate age of the quilt, is the number of cotton seeds remaining in the batting. Northern quilts made before the invention of the cotton gin by Eli Whitney in 1793 show more seeds than do quilts made in the South, where the slaves laboriously separated the seeds from the cotton.

Later, on the new frontiers, these regional differences became blurred. Pieced and appliqué patterns and quilting designs were exchanged among neighbors, and as the frontiers became settled communities and economic conditions improved, every quiltmaker attempted at least one appliqué quilt for "best" to display her needlework ability. Today, the midwestern farm women who carry on the tradition of quiltmaking still prefer the old pieced patterns such as the "Double Wedding Ring," the "Dresden Plate," and the "Drunkard's Path," although now that quiltmaking is a leisuretime activity instead of a necessity, the elaborate appliqué designs and the fancy-stitched "plain" quilts have gained in popularity.

Quiltmaking today is much easier with the conveniences of the sewing machine and the new synthetic fiberfill batting. In the early pioneer days, quilts were sometimes filled with leaves, grass, bark, or corn husks to provide warm bed coverings when cotton or wool were in short supply to use as quilt batting, and even these were not without disadvantages. Both cotton and wool batting separates and becomes lumpy after washing unless the rows of quilting stitches are very close, traditionally within one-fourth inch of each other. The lighter and more resilient fiberfill batting does not require such close quilting and therefore permits greater freedom in the quilting design. Quilts and comforters made with fiberfill also retain a puffy quality that adds another dimension to the patterns of color and form in the overall design. Many of the pieced quilt patterns can be made by sewing machine, and with the modern zigzag stitch attachment, appliqué work is easily done too. Setting together the block units of the quilt pattern or adding on the borders of the quilt by machine stitching rather than hand sewing saves time, and it is even possible to machine-quilt individual blocks by using techniques that will be discussed in a later chapter.

The contemporary experiments in quilting techniques, using the sewing machine and fiberfill batting, which have produced sculptured wall hangings and Claes Oldenburg stuffed "objects," may seem far removed from the old patchwork quilts, but in actuality they are an artistic adaptation of an ancient craft to today's life-style. For patch-work quilts themselves, although originally made to fill an eco-nomic need, developed into a creative outlet of tremendous importance for countless women and, not infrequently, men too. The Union soldier recuperating from wounds sustained in the Civil War and the midwest-ern farmer confined to a wheelchair by a physical illness discovered for themselves what generations of American women have known, that making a quilt can fulfill the deep need for personal self-expres-sion. Quilts reflect not only the economic and social circumstances of the quiltmaker, but more importantly, the quiltmaker's personal taste and innate sense of color and design. Even though the same quilt pat-terns have been repeated time and again by quiltmakers throughout the country, no two quilts have ever been alike. Each is the unique creation of one person's choice of colors, fabrics, and concept of the overall design. Like true artists, quiltmakers have used experiences from their personal lives as the subject matter for their quilts: familiar objects, the beauties of nature, aspects of pioneer life, and preoccupa-tions with religion and the political affairs of our country. Old quilts can be prized for their beauty and their antiquity, but for me they are creative social documents, testimonies, as vivid as the written word, to the lives of the women and men who made them.

FIG. 2–1. Central Illinois farm.

CHAPTER II
Pioneer Women

What makes American quilt designs so distinctive from their European counterparts is a vitality characteristic of the people who pioneered in the settlement of America (Fig. 2-1). The development of American quiltmaking, particularly the appliqué quilts, was of course influenced by the highly decorative, stylized European quilt designs, drawn from sources such as the beautiful needlework on lavish church vestments and the richly embroidered clothing worn by the wealthy. However, the American pieced quilts with their vivid colors and simple but bold designs are symbolic representations of the energetic pioneer spirit in confrontation with the rigors of frontier life. Living in difficult, often primitive, conditions and improvising with the materials at hand, the undaunted pioneer women created pieced quilts of great visual strength, which are part of our American heritage.

A fifth-generation descendant of Mennonite settlers in central Illinois, I was raised on stories of my forefathers who left Europe, seeking religious freedom, to homestead the prairies where they lie buried in tiny cemeteries carved out of the cornfields. I also grew up with a patchwork quilt on my bed, and assumed that quilts and quilting bees were commonplace everywhere until I lived in various cities in the United States and in Europe. Now, my interest in quiltmaking has led me home again, to a grateful appreciation of my family's history and traditional ways.

The opportunity to buy rich farmland for little money lured the men who settled the midwestern prairies less than 150 years ago, but the women who accompanied them had misgivings about their future homes on the new frontier. Rebecca Burlend, who emigrated from Yorkshire, England, to southern Illinois in 1831 with her husband and five small children, states quite frankly in her memoirs, "I gave up the idea of ending my days in my own country with the utmost reluctance, and should never have become an emigrant, if obedience to my husband's wishes had left me any alternative." Fearful of the unknown dangers that lay ahead and saddened by the prospect of leaving behind their relatives and friends, the pioneer women nevertheless packed up the few belongings they could take with them, including their treasured quilts, and followed where their menfolk led.

Traveling in crowded quarters on riverboats along the Ohio or the Mississippi, or in covered wagons through the sparsely settled, dense forests, the pioneers arrived at last on the fringe of the prairies that stretched ahead like an empty sea with perhaps a solitary clump of trees on the horizon. "I must say that I was sorely disappointed," commented Christiana Tillson about her first sight of the prairies. "Your father had talked so much about their beauty that I expected to feel a kind of enchantment. He said 'you never saw anything like this before.' I said 'no' but did not say I never saw anything more dismal and to those who have seen western prairies after the autumnal fires have passed over, leaving them in all their blackness, with an occasional strip of coarse grass or a scrubby bush, it will be needless to describe, and I think hard to gather beauties from it." Unfortunately for Mrs. Tillson, she had arrived on the prairies at the wrong season of the year. In the springtime, when a profusion of gaily colored flowers blossomed among the tall grasses, the sight greeting those early travelers was of unexpected beauty.

The prairie soil was unbelievably fertile and once the strongly rooted grasses had been turned under, it yielded luxurious crops of Indian corn and wheat. A new settler did not need to spend years cutting and burning trees or digging out rocks to clear his land; he could plant and harvest a crop the first year that he established a homestead. Small game, wild fowl, and fish were plentiful and wild grapes, plums, and luscious strawberries grew in abundance. The timber, a term used in Illinois for the woods that grew along the creeks and rivers on the edge of the grasslands, provided hickory and hazel nuts and wild honey for sweetening. Cultivated fruit trees, watermelons, pumpkins, and garden crops, all thrived in the rich soil.

It was a bountiful land, but nature exacted a heavy price for her gifts. The weather in the heart of the prairies was unpredictable and violent in its changes—terrifying lightning storms accompanied by torrential rains; hailstorms that destroyed a farmer's crops in minutes; and tornadoes, incredible in their destructiveness. In the summer, it was insufferable heat, stinging gnats, and drought. In midwinter, fierce blizzards and howling gales piled up snow into drifts higher than the hedgerows settlers used to fence off the fields. During the heavy spring rains the crude trails were turned into axle-deep mud and the creeks and rivers overflowed their banks. With homesteads so widely scattered, a family might not have a visitor for months on end. The pioneer woman left alone with small children while her husband journeyed to the nearest settlement for supplies had only her own stubborn determination and religious faith on which to rely.

Many of the immigrants who came to America from Europe were seeking the freedom to practice their religious beliefs as their consciences directed, and among them were my Mennonite ancestors. The Mennonites originated as a group called the Swiss Brethren at the time of the Reformation, and later took their formal name from a Dutch priest, Menno Simons, who was one of their early leaders. Convinced that the efforts to reform Christianity had not been carried far enough, the Mennonites separated from the mainstream of the Reformation on the doctrinal issue of infant baptism and were nicknamed "antibaptists" because of their conviction that only adults who voluntarily renounced their wrongdoings should be baptized and accepted into church membership. Mennonite doctrine is based on a literal interpretation of the Bible and an emphasis on the teachings of Christ, particularly the Sermon on the Mount. The Mennonites adopted a simplicity of life-style, and sought to live in peace with their fellowmen, adhering to the principle of nonviolence even at the cost of their own lives.

The Mennonites were persecuted and driven from one European country to another. Swiss Mennonites first moved to the German Palatinate and the Alsace-Lorraine region of France, then began emigrating to America in 1683 when William Penn offered them religious freedom in Pennsylvania. Dutch Mennonites went to northern Germany and Prussia in the 1600s and later to the Russian Ukraine. In 1874, many Russian Mennonites emigrated to Canada and the wheat states of Kansas and Nebraska where they introduced a hardy variety of Russian wheat, called Turkey red, which greatly increased wheat production in these areas. There are approximately 320,000 Mennonites in North America today, divided into some twenty branches within the Mennonite Church.

The Mennonites have retained their traditional emphasis on simplicity in dress, worship, and life-style, but today there is wide diversity in practice from the plain-dress Amish, who split off from the main body in the late seventeenth century, with their horses and buggies, to those Mennonites who dress in contemporary, albeit conservative, style and utilize the conveniences of modern times. Between these extremes in style of dress are the Mennonite women who still wear the traditional white prayer cap covering their simple hairstyles during worship services, and sometimes in daily life too, and the men who wear an ordinary suit with no necktie, or a plain coat with buttons straight to the neck and no lapels. However, a more important part of the Mennonite tradition than these surface differences in wearing apparel is their emphasis on family life and the brotherhood of the church community. Mennonites feel that it is not enough to profess a personal religious belief. They also must live their lives in good conscience toward their fellowmen, assisting each other in times of need.

My maternal great-great-grandparents, Christian and Barbara (Zimmerman) Reeser, and their three small children settled in Woodford County near Peoria, Illinois, in 1857. Christian was born in 1819 in France, but his parents were of Swiss and German descent so both German and French were spoken by the family. When France instituted compulsory military training, Christian's family decided to emigrate to Canada, having had favorable reports of the opportunities there from other Mennonite settlers. In 1838 or 1839, Christian with

FIG. 2–2. Christian Reeser on his hundredth birthday.

two older brothers and a sister left Le Havre on a ship bound for Canada. Since Christian was of draft age and was leaving the country illegally, he had to hide until the ship left French waters. Sixty-nine days later they landed in New Orleans, their ship having been buffeted by severe storms and blown off course as far south as the equator. In later years Christian liked to talk about that voyage across the Atlantic as being one of the most exciting experiences of his life.

The three brothers made their way to Butler County, Ohio, leaving their sister, who had married a fellow passenger, in New Orleans. They worked as farmhands for three years until they could save enough to buy land of their own in Delaware County, Indiana. By that time both of Christian's brothers had married. Christian, in anticipation of his own marriage, built a two-story log cabin with one room about 17 by 19 feet on each floor. He hewed the oak and beech logs by hand, and filled the cracks between the logs with oak chips and a mixture of clay and slaked lime. He had boards planed at the nearest sawmill to cover the log floor and hand-carved wooden pins to hold them together. The first story had two windows, the second boasted three, and the slanted roof was covered with planed clapboards. Christian was understandably proud of his handiwork, but his wife later liked to remind him that it may have been a fine home but it needed a thorough housecleaning when she arrived.

By all accounts, Christian Reeser was a remarkable man, known for his cheerful, optimistic nature, warm concern for his fellowmen, and good sense of humor. His religious beliefs were exemplified in his daily life, and at the age of forty-eight he accepted a call to the ministry. In those days, rural ministers were unpaid and to support his large family, which eventually numbered thirteen children, he continued to farm in between traveling long distances by horseback to preach a sermon or help a family in distress. Unlike many of his fellow Mennonites who believed in keeping themselves strictly apart from secular matters, Christian was very interested in both international affairs and the political happenings of this country. He had met Abraham Lincoln one time when both men were fording a river, and after that, he followed Lincoln's political career closely and several times traveled to hear him speak. A life-long Democrat, he made one exception—to vote for Lincoln for president. He cast his last vote when he was 101 years old, and died at the age of 103, steadfast in his religious faith to the end of his days.

Christian was quick to acknowledge that without his wife's courage and sacrifices he would not have been able to carry out his duties as a minister. Life as a pioneer wife and mother of a large family in trying financial circumstances was difficult for Barbara Zimmerman, who came from a financially secure, upper-class family in Baden, Germany. Barbara was well educated, unusual for a girl at that time, and after Christian's ordination, she taught him to read, for he had received little formal education. At the age of twenty, Barbara left her parents' home much against their wishes to follow her German fiancé to Philadelphia, but she refused to marry him until she repaid the money he had spent for her boat fare. She found a job keeping house for a family with fourteen children, and later was happy to accept an invitation to live with her two brothers who were homesteading in Indiana. There she met and fell in love with thirty-three-year-old Christian Reeser, whom she married when she was twenty-one and only after she had paid her debt to her former fiancé in Philadelphia. Only once in later years did Barbara's children hear her mention this man who had prospered in business, and wonder aloud if her life would have been easier had she married him instead of a minister who sacrificed the comfort of his family to the needs of others. Barbara,

FIG. 2–3. Portrait of author's great-grandmother, Ann Maria Reeser Ulrich (second from right, first row) and her family. Her great-aunt Fanny Ulrich Schrock is at the extreme right, top row.

too, was a remarkable woman who faced the future with courage and a determination to make the best of whatever circumstances she encountered.

The first three of Barbara and Christian's thirteen children, including my great-grandmother, Anna Marie, were born in the log cabin in Indiana. By that time Christian had concluded that it would take too long to clear enough of the densely timbered land he owned to earn more than a bare livelihood, and he and his brother decided to move their families to Illinois. Barbara's youngest child was three weeks old when the two families set out in covered wagons. The trails were badly marked so travel was slow, and the weather was very hot and water supplies scarce. Everyone suffered from thirst, and the new baby cried with hunger because he was unable to nurse. When they finally arrived in Illinois, Barbara determined that she would never move again, although Christian was always intrigued by the lure of rich, cheap land to be found farther west.

The land that Christian purchased in Woodford County, Illinois, had a small log house and stable on it but both were badly in need of repair, so Christian set about building the house that was to be their home for forty years until he retired from farming. Barbara spent the last years of her life in relative comfort living in town. Although additions were later made, the original house was two stories divided into four rooms. The ground floor had a small bedroom and a large kitchen with a big black cooking range, and this room was the center of all of the family's indoor activities. Here, during the long winter evenings, Christian and his sons made tools and farm equipment, and molded lead bullets for use against the wolves that preyed on the farm animals. Here Barbara mended and sewed, and read aloud from the Bible and the few other books they had. Summer evenings were spent outdoors on the long porch that fronted the house. A hand-split rail fence enclosed the yard and the front gate was framed by the woodpile on one side and the "slop" barrel on the other, much to the annoyance of Christian's daughters who never could persuade their father to move it to a less conspicuous spot. The cellar of the house, which was entered from outdoors, served as a pantry and cold storage for the potato bin, the sauerkraut barrel, the cider and wine barrels, and the shelves of winter apples, and also was a place of refuge during the severe storms. As the years went by, a larger barn, a summer kitchen, a smokehouse, and small buildings for the livestock were added to the property.

With so much work to be done in cultivating the land, the Reeser children began working long hours in the fields with their parents when they were very young. Barbara carried her newest baby tied to her back, afraid to leave him lying on the ground because of the many snakes. After the birth of her seventh child, the family's financial situation improved enough so that they were able to hire men to help out during the busy seasons, and Barbara's work was then confined to the never-ending task of caring for her large family. Of her thirteen children, only one did not survive infancy—an unusual record for those days of high infant mortality. Sometimes a midwife was called in, but Christian considered himself as adept as anyone in helping at the delivery of his children and he often did so unaided.

To support his increasing family, Christian gradually acquired more land, which provided a self-sustaining livelihood for the family. The problem was to acquire enough cash to buy certain foodstuffs, cloth, and other articles that could not be produced on the farm. Barbara churned the extra cream from their small herd of cows into butter, which she traded at a nearby town, and she also sold hens and eggs to the traveling peddlers who periodically visited the farm. Most of the food she prepared was home grown, and with plenty of fresh vegetables, eggs, milk and cream, and home-butchered meat, the family was well fed. Barbara preserved food for the winter months by drying corn, beans, and fruits, and by storing cabbage, carrots, and turnips in a barrel sunk in the garden to keep the contents from freezing. Sauerkraut, pickled beets and cucumbers, relishes, and fresh-ground horseradish in early spring provided the "sours" beloved by those of German descent. Sugar was too expensive for daily use but there were plenty of "sweets"—fruit pies, cakes, and cookies filled with nuts and raisins and flavored with sorghum or molasses. Gallons of homemade apple butter were eaten with the bread that Barbara baked twice a week, and grape jelly and fruit jams were served for company dinner.

Once a year, usually in late December, the family butchered seven or eight hogs, a steer or two, and perhaps a sheep. Butchering was hard work and the neighbors helped to scrape and clean the carcasses and cut up the meat. Hog hams and shoulders were soaked in brine for several weeks, then hung in the smokehouse and cured with hickory smoke. Bony meat pieces were fried and stored in large crocks covered with lard, a method that preserved the meat for a long time. All the trimmings were ground into sausage that was encased in the hog intestines after the women had finished the unpleasant task of scraping them clean. No portion of the carcass was wasted. Liverwurst was made from the ground mixture of head meat, ears, tongue, and parts of the heart and liver; the hog's stomach was served with a bread dressing; and the feet and ears were made into a jellied meat dish. Dried beef and sausages made of a mixture of beef and pork were also cured in the smokehouse beside the slabs of bacon and the hams. A major task in the butchering process was the preparation or "rendering" of lard, which was the only shortening used for cooking. Cubes of fat were boiled in a kettle over an open fire until the cracklings rose, then cooled and put through the lard press. The finished product was stored in large crocks in the cellar.

The meat supply was supplemented by fried or roasted chicken, by the wild ducks, geese, and quail that the boys hunted, and by rabbits and squirrels. Christian was fond of fishing and frequently took the boys to a nearby river to catch a mess of fish for the family dinner. Good food was plentiful on the Reeser table but many hours went into the preparation of the meals. When the neighboring men were helping out with butchering or grain harvesting, Barbara often had as many as twenty or more hungry people to feed.

Food preparation was only one of Barbara's chores. Wash day must have been sheer drudgery. Gallons of water had to be pumped, carried to the cooking range to be heated, and carried back to the washtubs. What backaches must have resulted from having to bend over those tubs scrubbing the clothes on a washboard. All the soap for both laundry and personal needs was made at home. Several times a year the waste fats Barbara had carefully saved were put into a kettle and boiled with a lye solution made by pouring water through the wood ashes accumulated in the cooking range. The boiled mass that was cooled and cut into blocks produced an effective soap still being made for laundry purposes today by some people in rural communities.

With washing such backbreaking toil, clothing was not washed as frequently as it is today, and dark colors were chosen for everyday wear. Barbara used walnut shells to dye the homespun yarn that she knitted into stockings as walnuts produce a practical greenish-brown color. There were two spinning wheels, a large homemade one without a treadle and a smaller one for spinning finer wools, and enough yarn was spun to keep the family supplied with stockings, scarves, and sweaters. Making all the clothing was an enormous task but some of Barbara's burden was relieved when a sewing machine, one of the first in that area, was purchased seventeen years after the family settled in Illinois. The first garments made on it, my great-grandmother's black silk dress and my great-grandfather's white shirt for their wedding day, were so successful that Barbara was convinced she had made a good decision in spending the large sum of seventy dollars for the sewing machine.

For years, Barbara saved cotton rags until she finally had enough to make a carpet for the downstairs bedroom. The rags were sewed into long strips that were taken to a carpet weaver in a nearby town. The new carpet was laid over a layer of fresh hay, which provided a place for the dust to settle. At spring and fall housecleaning, the hay was removed, the floor scrubbed, and new hay was put down. Barbara and the girls enjoyed the luxury of that rag carpet but Christian worried about the possibility of fire and never could reconcile himself to having a layer of hay underfoot in his bedroom.

Wool from sheep raised on the farm was taken to the nearest carder to be made into batting for quilts and comforters. Although wool was generally considered to be too expensive to use for quilt batting, it was more economical for the Reeser family, who raised their own, than would have been the purchase of cotton. None of Barbara's quilts and comforters has survived to the present time; they simply were worn out by the large family over years of hard use. However, a beautifully stitched sampler, made by Barbara during her childhood in Germany, has been handed down in the family.

Barbara Reeser died at the age of seventy-two, and at the time of Christian's death twenty years later, their descendants numbered 11 surviving children, 82 grandchildren, and 101 great-grandchildren. Her life is best summed up by the words from Proverbs, Chapter 31, verses 27 and 28: "She looketh well to the ways of her household, and eateth not the bread of idleness. Her children arise up, and call her blessed; her husband also, and he praiseth her."

One of Barbara Reeser's granddaughters, noted as a skilled quilt-maker among women who have carried on the traditional craft, is my great-aunt, Fanny Ulrich Schrock. Unfortunately, Aunt Fanny's health and eyesight are failing now that she is eighty-three years old, but until a year or so ago she was always piecing still another quilt to add to the hundreds she has made. One of her favorite patterns, the "Golden Glow," is shown in A in the color section. This exquisite quilt is a challenge for even an experienced quiltmaker to piece, as each eight-point star in the pattern is made with a gathered eight-petaled flower at its center. It was the "Golden Glow" quilt that Aunt Fanny had made for me that I remembered when I was living abroad and decided that I too wanted to learn the craft of making patchwork quilts.

CHAPTER III
Quilt Auctions and Quilting Bees

The quilt auctions that are part of the annual Mennonite Relief Sales held throughout the United States and Canada may be the only auctions in the world that are customarily opened with a prayer and an admonition to the prospective buyers: "Bid as you feel you are led by the Lord." Even the professional auctioneers donate their services, for all the proceeds of the Relief Sales go to the Mennonite Central Committee, a relief agency that provides food, medical care, agricultural assistance, and educational programs around the world. The quilts and comforters are made by Mennonite churchwomen working together throughout the year at quilting frames set up in their home churches. The residents of the Mennonite Homes for the Aged also contribute quilts to the auctions, as do individual quiltmakers. At the 1973 auction held by the central Illinois congregations, nearly fifty quilts and comforters were sold, all of them hand-quilted and many large enough for today's queen-size beds.

Quilt lovers come from far away to attend the auctions, for there are quilts to satisfy everyone's personal taste. Such favorite old pieced patterns as the "Nine-Patch," the "Double Wedding Ring," and the "Prairie Queen" vie for attention with the varieties of tulip and of rose appliqué designs. And the elaborately stitched feather wreath and rose wreath designs of the "plain" quilts are anything but plain. Also popular are the embroidered quilts such as the cross-stitched wreath design made by an eighty-six-year-old grandmother that sold for $250. A queen-size "plain" quilt with matching pillows brought the highest price of $300, and the average price of the twenty highest-priced quilts was $171.75, real bargains for quilt collectors by today's standards. The quilts and comforters are only a part of the handmade items for sale. There are knitted afghans, stuffed toys, rag rugs, baby clothes, cross-stitched aprons and towels, and a variety of other needlework and crafts, all made by the Mennonite women. "Nothing store-boughten here!"

Another feature of the Relief Sales is the "eat all you want" breakfast of homemade sausage and pancakes, which was served to 4,470 people at the 1973 Illinois sale. Volunteers from the member congregations butchered 86 donated hogs, and made 6½ tons of whole pork sausage, which was for sale along with spareribs and fresh liver sausage. Other gastronomical delights were to be found in the Dutch Market—fresh pretzels and home-baked bread, homemade shoofly and Dutch apple pies, and home-canned pickles. The adventuresome could sample chowchow, a mixed vegetable relish; scrapple, a dish made of fried liver pudding and cornmeal; or cuply kase, a kind of sour, smooth cottage cheese—some of the many traditional Swiss-German delicacies. The aroma of hot raised sugar doughnuts permeated the air, and little wonder, as 1,200 dozen doughnuts were made and sold. An estimated 15,000 people attended the 1973 Illinois sale, and approximately $45,000 was raised for relief.

Making quilts for the annual Relief Sales is not the only way that Mennonite churchwomen utilize quilting bees to raise funds. They do custom quilting for those people who have been fortunate enough to inherit an old quilt top or find one tucked away in a piece of antique furniture. Also, many women who enjoy making a pieced or appliquéd quilt top prefer to have the actual quilting done by experienced hands. The Ladies Aid groups of the individual congregations meet once a month from September to June for an all-day quilting bee (Fig. 3-1). The prices they charge for custom quilting vary according to the complexity of the quilting design, and further information on custom quilting and the annual quilt auctions can be obtained from The Material Aid Director, Mennonite Central Committee, 21 South 12th Street, Akron, Pennsylvania 17501.

For these Mennonite farm women, keeping busy with useful work

FIG. 3–1. Monthly quilting bee held by the Ladies Aid of the Mennonite Church, Meadows, Illinois.

is an ingrained habit. Even during their winter vacations in Florida, the Mennonite women join together to make quilts and knot comforters for the relief programs as they would ordinarily do at their home congregations. To their way of thinking, retirement from the labors of farm life provides the opportunity to devote even more time to their volunteer projects. One of these active volunteers is Mrs. Mattie Bachman, an accomplished quiltmaker, who for the past fifteen years has been in charge of the quilting projects undertaken at the Maplelawn Home for senior citizens in Eureka, Illinois (Fig. 3-2). Although she has raised a large family and passed the age when most people feel they deserve to take life easy, Mrs. Bachman is still too busy helping others to be considered "retired."

With the assistance of Mrs. Bachman and volunteers like her, quilting bees are held five afternoons a week at the Maplelawn Home (Fig. 3-3). The residents of the home not only donate quilts to the annual Relief Sales, but also fill custom quilting orders and always have more advance orders than they can finish in a year's time. The money that they earn through custom quilting, along with the fall craft sale of individually made handwork, goes toward the purchase

FIG. 3–2. (*above*) Mrs. Mattie Bachman, quiltmaker and volunteer.

FIG. 3–3. (*below*) Quilting bee at the Maplelawn Home, Eureka, Illinois.

of supplies and new equipment for the arts and crafts department, providing the residents with a well-deserved sense of their own accomplishments. In the past, classes have been held to which women came from miles around to learn the traditional skills of quilting from these ladies who hold advanced degrees as experienced quiltmakers.

The Mennonites feel that aid to others is best expressed through the concrete efforts of their own hands, whether it be rebuilding a neighbor's barn that has burned down, canning food and making quilts for the hungry and the homeless, or sending trained volunteers to reconstruct homes in devastated areas. They also believe in the importance of helping others to help themselves by providing the necessary materials, tools, and technical assistance through Mennonite Central Committee projects. One of these self-help projects is Hill 'n Hollow Crafts, a program in Kentucky that provides materials at cost for women who make quilts and other handcrafts to sell to markets located for them through the project. Living in isolated areas and subsisting on below-poverty-level incomes, these women did not have the opportunity to use their skills for their financial benefit until the self-help project provided them with the necessary means to earn a better standard of living for their families.

The Mennonites as a group are an anomaly within present-day American society but in clinging to their own traditional ways, they are helping to preserve a part of our heritage. Quiltmaking and related handcrafts still exist today because of people like the Mennonites who have never forgotten the importance of working with one's own hands to create objects of visual beauty. And the quilting bees held by the Mennonite women are not merely a quaint custom, but a vital manifestation of that spirit of neighborly cooperation that undergirded the settlement of America.

Both Christiana Tillson and Rebecca Burlend mention in their memoirs how desperately lonely they were during the early years of their lives on the frontier. Pioneer society was largely masculine; the bachelors far outnumbered married men with families and the arrival of a new bride or new family in the area was greeted with great excitement and curiosity. Starved for female companionship, the women eagerly looked forward to a quilting bee, one of the rare opportunities when they could share in woman's talk. They would arrive early in the morning at the hostess's home and spend the day, talking as fast as their fingers stitched the quilts. Their menfolk joined them for a big supper followed by an evening of conversation, games, and dancing, if the religious convictions of the hostess permitted. New neighbors became acquainted, opinions and ideas were exchanged, and community projects were organized.

Quilting bees also afforded an opportunity for courtship, as immortalized by Stephen Foster in his song lyrics, "And 'twas from Aunt Dinah's quilting party, I was seeing Nellie home." Later, when the young couple had reached an understanding, the prospective bride often held a quilting bee for her bridal quilt as the official announcement of her engagement. This was the occasion for her to display her trousseau, including the baker's dozen quilts that she was expected to have finished by the time she reached marriageable age. Her bridal quilt was of course the most treasured of all, and there were many superstitions concerning it. In some parts of the country, it was considered bad luck for the bride-to-be to even make her own bridal quilt, and the custom of her friends' making a quilt for her as a wedding present developed. Usually each friend made an individual block in the quilt design on which she embroidered or signed her name as a remembrance of their friendship. At the quilting bee, the prospective bride was allowed to "snap" the quilt, that is, to snap the chalk-covered string that made a mark across the quilt for the quilting pattern, but she was not permitted to work on the quilting herself.

Social gatherings known as friendship quilt parties were held by the young girls not yet of marriageable age. Each girl brought scraps of her old dresses to make a quilt block that was embroidered with her name and the date. The finished blocks were set together and presented to one member of the group who in turn gave a quilting bee to finish the friendship quilt, thus providing the opportunity for two parties, which livened up the daily routine.

Another expression of friendship was the "presentation" quilt frequently made by churchwomen for the minister of their congregation or his wife. The quilt in Figs. 3-4 and 3-5 was made forty years ago by community friends for the wife of a Mennonite minister and each

FIGS. 3–4 & 3–5. "Presentation" quilt, and a detail, made for a Mennonite minister's wife.

block is embroidered with the name of the woman who pieced it. Often the friendship and the presentation quilts were made up of a variety of block patterns that created a rather chaotic overall appearance, but in the quilt shown, each block is the same pattern although every quiltmaker used a different print for her block. Like the bridal quilts, these friendship quilts were treasured by their owners and carefully handed on to the next generation.

Quilting bees held to raise funds for church activities were a common practice in the nineteenth century and continued in the rural areas of the country well into the present century. Whether as an opportunity for communal activity or an excuse for a social get-together, the quilting bee was an important event for our great-grandmothers, whose lives were limited by social conventions to their homes and their churches. But as the social conditions in America changed so that women could begin to envision new roles for themselves, it is not surprising that Susan B. Anthony found attentive audiences at quilting bees for some of her early lectures on woman suffrage.

CHAPTER IV
Quilt Design

Confronted with the problem of making a warm bed covering from the contents of her scrap bag, the pioneer housewife simply stitched together the odd-shaped patches of cloth until she had a piece large enough to cover her bed, and she named her new creation the "crazy quilt." Despite its name, a crazy quilt usually showed some degree of organization in that the patches were cut into relatively the same size and the colors balanced out to the extent that the limited contents of the scrap bag permitted. Of necessity, however, the crazy quilt was a hodgepodge of materials—homespun linsey-woolsey, precious cotton prints, rough jeans fabric, woolens, and whatever else the scrap bag contained at the time. The crazy-quilt design became popular again during the Victorian era but this time crazy quilts were made from silks, velvets, and brocades, elaborately embroidered and pieced together with decorative stitching. These often frivolous concoctions were not intended for functional use as bed coverings, but instead they graced the parlor sofa as an ornamental "slumber throw." Details from two crazy quilts made in the Victorian style by farm women are shown in Figs. 4-1, 4-2, and 4-3; one is embroidered with the date 1892 and the other has two embroidered dates, '94, and '96, indicating the beginning and completion of the work. Both display embroidered figures and featherstitching, but in contrast to the typical slumber throws of the period, these crazy quilts are made from more

FIG. 4–1. (*above*) Detail from a crazy quilt made in 1892.

FIGS. 4–2 & 4–3. (*below*) Details from a crazy quilt completed in 1896.

durable fabrics—some silks and velvets but many more pieces of fine woolens, in darker colors, characteristic of the plain dress of the Mennonite farm women who made them. The first of these was made by sewing the odd-shaped patches into wide strips and setting them together with strips of a solid color to form a striped effect. The other was made by framing the squares of odd-shaped patches in a windowpane effect. Both are good design ideas, for a quilt top composed entirely of odd-shaped patches is confusing to the eye, and less sewing is required, too, if there are fewer patches to be pieced together.

When the quiltmaker had enough large patches of cloth in her scrap bag, she cut them into a uniform shape to piece together her quilt top. The hexagon shape was frequently used as an overall design in old quilts like the "Century" pattern shown in Fig. 4-4. Every patch in this quilt is made of a different print, predominantly brown, but pink and rose prints are randomly scattered among the darker prints, many of which have small pink figures in them. A more complex design, using uniformly shaped patches, was created by grouping together the colors of the patches to form design units within the overall design. Pictured in Fig. 4-5 is a traditional "Flower Garden" pattern composed of hexagonal patches, but in this design the colored prints are grouped to form individual "flower beds" set together with white patches and the green of the garden walk. The quilt shown in Fig. 4-6 is another version of the same pattern known as the "Dime-Size Flower Garden" because the tiny hexagonal patches measure only seven-eighths of an inch along each side. Piecing this quilt was a real test of the quiltmaker's skill and patience, for these tiny patches are extremely difficult to work with, yet every patch fits together with perfectly pointed corners.

Pieced quilts made from a single uniform shape—squares, or rectangles, or equilateral triangles, or hexagons—are known as one-patch designs. In experimenting with her scraps of cloth, the quiltmaker discovered that a variety of two-patch designs could be formed by simply cutting a square diagonally across the corner into triangles, and combining the square and triangles in different positions. "Birds

FIG. 4–4. (*above left*) "Century" pieced quilt made before 1877.

FIG. 4–5. (*below*) Traditional "Flower Garden" pieced quilt.

FIG. 4–6. (*above right*) "Dime-Size Flower Garden" pieced quilt.

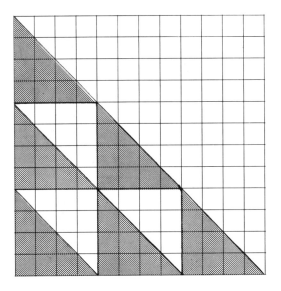

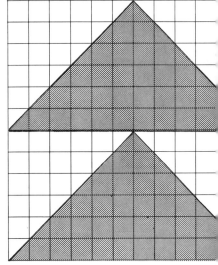

FIG. 4–7. (*upper left*) "Birds in the Air."

FIG. 4–8. (*above*) "Wild-Goose Chase."

FIG. 4–9. (*left*) "Saw Tooth" pieced quilt.

in the Air" (Fig. 4-7) and "Wild-Goose Chase" (Fig. 4-8) are two-patch designs frequently seen in old quilts. The "Saw Tooth" quilt shown in Fig. 4-9 also is basically a two-patch design composed of right-angle triangles, although it appears to be more complex. Pieced-quilt designs are not difficult to figure out if you keep in mind that the basic block unit is a square. No matter how complex the design

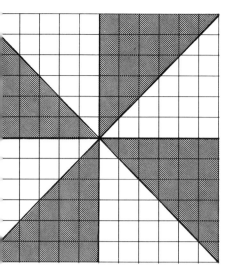

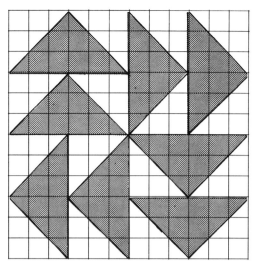

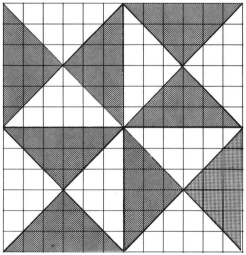

FIG. 4–10. (*above*) "Windmill."

FIG. 4–11. (*upper right*) "Dutchman's Puzzle."

FIG. 4–12. (*right*) "Yankee Puzzle."

may appear to be, the various geometric shapes of which it is composed must fit together in the square block unit.

Four-patch designs, of which the old pattern variously named in different parts of the country the "Windmill," "Water Wheel," "Mill Wheel," and "Pin Wheel" (Fig. 4-10) is an example, are simply block designs that can be divided horizontally and vertically into four smaller equal squares. The more complex patterns known as "Dutchman's Puzzle" (Fig. 4-11) and "Yankee Puzzle" (Fig. 4-12) are two simple adaptations of the "Windmill" pattern. Among the four-patch designs, two star patterns, "Clay's Choice" (Fig. 4-13), named in honor of Henry Clay, and the "Blazing Star" (Fig. 4-14), are frequently seen on old quilt tops.

A basic "Nine-Patch" block design is a square divided into nine equal squares. Well-known variations of this design are the "Shoofly" (Fig. 4-15), "Duck and Ducklings" (Fig. 4-16), and "Philadelphia Pavement" (Fig. 4-17), and a wide variety of other designs can be made by rearranging the light and dark squares or by dividing the individual squares into triangles. The quilt pictured in Fig. 4-18 is called an "Improved Nine-Patch" and is rather demanding to piece because the four corners of the basic nine-patch are pointed rather than squared and the unit blocks are set together with melon-shaped pieces to form an overall pattern of interlocking circles. The overall pattern forms scalloped edges along three sides of the quilt but the quiltmaker has squared off the top edge because it will not be visible when the quilt is on a bed.

Also included among the nine-patch designs is the "Variable Star"

FIG. 4–13. (*below left*) "Clay's Choice."

FIG. 4–14. (*below right*) "Blazing Star."

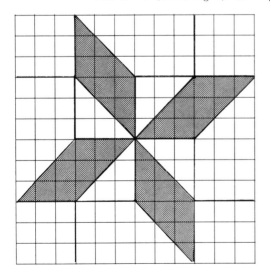
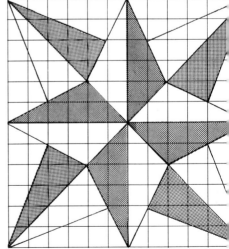

FIG. 4–15. (*top left*) "Shoofly."

FIG. 4–16. (*top right*) "Duck and Ducklings."

FIG. 4–17. (*lower left*) "Philadelphia Pavement."

FIG. 4–18. (*lower right*) "Improved Nine-Patch" pieced quilt.

pattern (Fig. 4-19), which is the basis for many of the star variations. The "Rising Star" (Fig. 4-20) is one of the more popular variations seen on old quilts. The portion of the quilt shown in D in the color

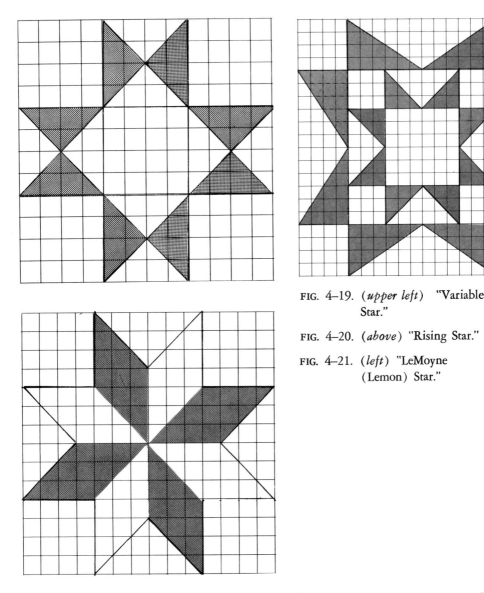

FIG. 4–19. (*upper left*) "Variable Star."

FIG. 4–20. (*above*) "Rising Star."

FIG. 4–21. (*left*) "LeMoyne (Lemon) Star."

section is another variation set with a pin wheel in the center and called simply the "Pieced Star."

Another basic pattern in quilt block design is the eight-point star formed by dividing a square into eight diamonds. This is the famous "Star of LeMoyne," named after Jean Baptiste LeMoyne, who founded New Orleans in 1718. In the North, the "LeMoyne Star" was renamed the "Lemon Star" (Fig. 4-21), which was both easier to pronounce and less reminiscent of the French ownership of the Louisiana territory before it was incorporated into the United States in 1803. The

FIG. 4–22. "Cottage Tulip" pieced quilt.

"LeMoyne Star" is the basis for all the pieced lily and tulip patterns, including the "Cottage Tulip" (Fig. 4-22). The "Cottage Tulip" design requires considerable skill on the part of the quiltmaker, for the design is entirely pieced although it appears to be appliqué work. The eight-point star is surrounded by eight pieced tulips and their leaves, which form a circular medallion, pieced together with wedge-shaped patches to complete the square of the block unit.

In most of the eight-point-star patterns, the block unit is completed by squares and right-angle triangles set alternately between the diamond points of the stars. However, the star can be built up to any size by continuing to set two diamonds in each of the right angles formed by the preceding row, and in the very old pattern known as the "Star of Bethlehem" or the "Rising Sun," one big star often covered the entire surface of the quilt top. In D in the color section, nine stars of Bethlehem were set together to form the total design. In G of the color section is another eight-point-star design called the "Star of Hope," each block of which is pieced in a medallion effect and the blocks set together with the "Saw Tooth" pattern.

Pieced six-point-diamond-star patterns were not as popular as the eight-point star because it is more difficult to cut a six-point star from a square, and then, too, hexagons are needed to square off the block unit. In H in the color section is shown an unusual example of a pieced six-point-star quilt known as the "Evening Star." The quilt-maker chose to finish off the long sides of the quilt as scalloped edges rather than to square the unit blocks by setting in hexagons, and the scallops add the finishing touch to a masterful piece of quiltmaking.

Piecing a star pattern is demanding because the overall design can be easily thrown off balance if the diamond points in the pattern do not fit together exactly, and these patterns were rightfully considered advanced quiltmaking. A beginning quiltmaker would be wise to choose one of the less difficult pieced patterns such as the famous "Log Cabin" quilt (Fig. 5-4), a pattern that also can be easily made on a sewing machine. The "Log Cabin" is based on a small central square surrounded by rectangular-shaped "logs" of varying lengths, the light-colored logs placed on one side of the unit block and the dark-colored ones on the other. Variations of the basic pattern depend on the way that the light–dark colors of the individual blocks are set together in an overall design. In the "Barn Raising," the colors form diamond patterns, and in "Straight Furrow" or "Sunlight and Shadow," the colors form diagonal stripes across the quilt top.

Another variation of the "Log Cabin" is the "Pineapple" (Fig. 4-23), in which the logs are trapezoidal in shape instead of rectangular. One of the few quilts made by a man that I've seen was a "Pineapple" pattern made by a Chicago tailor in 1908 as a wedding present for his new daughter-in-law. He used scraps of men's wool suiting, predominantly light and dark gray, but he put a bright red center in each block unit. The quilt was made on a sewing machine using a technique known as making a "pressed" quilt. The center square of the block was basted into position on a foundation fabric, then the trapezoid-shaped pieces were seamed on and turned back over each side and the raw edge caught by the seam of the next patch. Technically speaking, the tailor's quilt is neither a quilt nor a comforter as it has no batting and is not stitched together, but since he

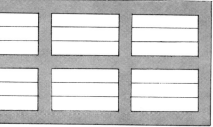

FIG. 4–23. (*upper left*) "Pineapple."

FIG. 4–24. (*left*) "Roman Square."

FIG. 4–25. (*above*) "Zig-Zag."

went to the trouble of piecing a "Pineapple" pattern for the top, he certainly deserves credit for having made a quilt.

"Roman Square" (Fig. 4-24) and "Zig-Zag" (Fig. 4-25), two old patterns that fall into the category of the three-patch designs, are also easy to sew and strikingly contemporary in feeling, depending on the color combinations of which they are made. Each block of the "Roman Square" is formed of three variously colored oblong patches, and the blocks are set together in a framework of a solid color. This design, like the crazy quilt, was revived during the Victorian era to make slumber throws of colorful silks and fine wools crossbarred in black. The "Zig-Zag" design is made by cutting a light and dark square in a diagonal from the center of one side to the opposite corner and setting the light and dark triangles together as shown in the diagram.

A very common old pattern called the "Chimney Sweep" (Fig. 4-26) is another pattern that is easy to sew because it is composed simply of five rows of squares set together with small triangles to complete the block unit. The trick to making a visually exciting quilt, using a relatively simple pattern, lies in the contrast of colored and patterned fabrics used. In the quilt shown, the pieced blocks are made from a variety of gold and reddish-brown prints, and gold and green plaids, which are set off by a background of gold-and-white-checked gingham. Another effective way to use this simple design is to piece a chain of thirteen rows of squares and set the pieced blocks together in a framework of a solid color, giving the impression of vividly colored stained-glass windows.

The "Chimney Sweep" is a close cousin to the very popular "Irish Chain" pattern, which is also composed of rows of squares, but in the "Irish Chain" the pieced blocks are set together with plain white blocks. The ladies at the quilting bee pictured in Fig. 3-1 are quilting a "Single Irish Chain," which is simply a basic nine-patch set together with white blocks. There also are Double and Triple Irish Chain patterns, and the quilt shown in D in the color section is a complex variation that is called, not the Irish Chain to the 13th degree, but "Quilt of a Thousand Prints." To tie together the overall design of this quilt, each of the pieced blocks is bordered by a row of green and a row of red squares, and the entire quilt is framed by a green and a red border.

Another popular old pattern is "Boxes" or "Baby's Blocks" (Fig. 4-27), so named because the diamond patches that make up the pattern create an optical illusion of piled-up blocks. Other old names

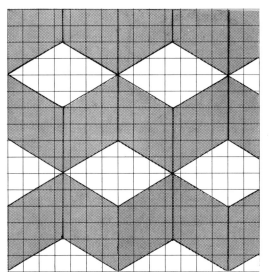

FIG. 4–26. (*opposite page, top*) Detail from "Chimney Sweep" pieced quilt.

FIG. 4–27. (*left*) "Baby's Blocks."

FIG. 4–28. (*opposite page, lower*) "World's Puzzle" pieced quilt, also known as "Solomon's Puzzle" and the "Drunkard's Path."

for this pattern were "Pandora's Box" and also "Heavenly Stairs" because by shading the colors selected, the effect of a flight of stairs could be created. The diamond patches must be pieced together precisely in order to maintain the optical illusion, and the pattern is most effective when there is a distinct contrast in the colors used.

Setting together the pattern of the quilt pictured in Fig. 4-28 must be as confusing as the variety of names by which it is known. The owner of the quilt shown called it the "World's Puzzle," but another quiltmaker said it was "Solomon's Puzzle," and yet a third called it the "Drunkard's Path." Very old quilts of this design are also called "Robbing Peter to Pay Paul," probably because the basic block unit consists of a "robbed" white square compensated with a quarter-circle patch cut from a dark square, and vice versa (Fig. 4-29). To add to the confusion, there are at least twelve variations of this pattern. The ladies pictured in Fig. 3-3 are quilting one variation called the "Baseball," and two others, "Falling Timbers" and "Love Ring," are shown in Figs. 4-30 and 4-31. It's fun to figure out with a pencil and piece of paper how many different variations you can come up with.

Pieced patterns that are formed by circular-shaped patches are much more difficult to sew together smoothly than the straight-edge patterns composed of squares, triangles, or diamonds. The "Orange Peel" or "Compass" quilt shown in Fig. 4-32 is definitely a work of postgraduate quiltmaking, for not only do all the patches have rounded edges but great care also must be taken in setting the patches together to maintain the overall design. At first glance, the quilt shown in Fig. 4-33, which is an adaptation of the old pattern known as "World Without End," appears to be equally as complex as the "Orange Peel," but this pattern is composed of squares, triangles, and diamonds although it creates an illusion of interlocking circles. Because of the difficulty of piecing curved patches, some patterns like the "Dresden Plate" quilt (C in the color section) and the "Basket" quilt (D in the color section) were first pieced together and then appliquéd on the background material.

Old appliqué quilts show a greater freedom of design than do the pieced quilts because appliqué pieces were cut from whole cloth to make a planned design rather than built up of whatever scraps of cloth were available. Also, the quiltmaker was not limited by consideration of geometric forms in planning her appliqué design as it is much easier to appliqué curved pieces than to seam them together. Many more old appliqué quilts than pieced ones are found in the collections of museums and historical societies because they were intended for display as the quiltmaker's "best" counterpane and did not receive the wear and tear of everyday use. Some of these counterpanes are very wide, as much as four feet across, and were made to

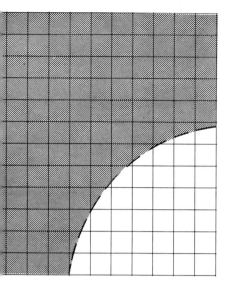

FIG. 4–29. (*upper left*) "Drunkard's Path."

FIG. 4–30. (*above*) "Falling Timbers."

FIG. 4–31. (*left*) "Love Ring."

cover the big old four-poster beds with all the extra feather mattresses in the household stored on top. Often the old appliqué quilts were intended as the bridal quilt to complete the traditional baker's dozen quilts of a young lady's trousseau.

The appliqué quilts that have survived from the eighteenth century are fantastic creations of exotic birds and bouquets of flowers carefully cut from colorful India chintz patterns and appliquéd to the background with exquisite needlework. The hand-painted and wax-

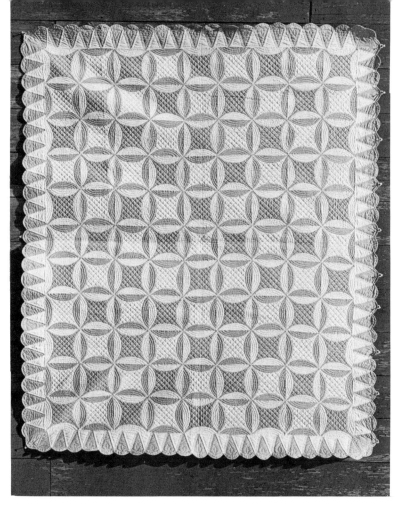

FIG. 4–32. "Orange Peel" or "Compass" pieced quilt.

resist dyed India chintzes, introduced into Europe as early as 1630, were highly prized by women whose dresses were made of drab woolens, for the chintzes were far less expensive than the colorful silks and velvets that only the wealthy could afford. India shawls and oriental carpets also were among the treasures brought back by the ships engaged in the East India trade. All served as inspirations for appliqué quilt designs, which were planned as an entire unit, usually with a large central medallion framed by a series of different borders, both appliquéd and pieced. Indeed, the overall effect was that of an oriental carpet. It seems surprising to find peacocks, pomegranates, and Persian pears, known as the "pickle pear" among quiltmakers,

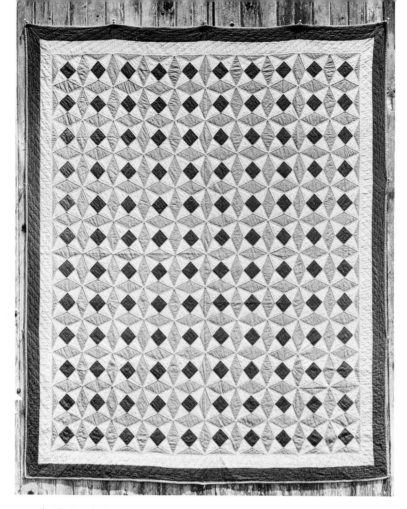

FIG. 4–33. Variation of the "World Without End" pieced quilt.

on old appliqué quilts but these motifs were typically part of the designs of the India chintzes. Some of the very old appliqué quilts made in America were designed to represent the "tree of life," an Eastern symbol of immortality depicting a stylized tree with birds and butterflies in its branches, human figures standing on a mound of earth at its base, and a background of randomly scattered bunches of flowers.

The India chintzes were so popular that the manufacture of cotton prints, hand-printed from carved wooden blocks, was quickly established in both England and France. At the end of the eighteenth century, a faster process for printing cottons using incised copper plates was developed in France, and these new prints, named "toiles de Jouy," from the town where they originated, became the rage for bed coverings, hangings, upholstery and curtain materials. The earliest toiles de Jouy· were printed in monotone colors of pink, blue, brown, or puce on white, and featured large designs of historical or allegorical scenes and luxurious floral bouquets from which the quiltmakers carefully cut out the intricate details and appliquéd them on quilt tops.

One of the favorite designs for an appliqué quilt was the "Garden." It had a central medallion of flowers surrounded by birds, nosegays, ribbons, and sometimes flower- and fruit-filled baskets. No two of these Garden quilts were alike and the success of the overall design depended on the individual quiltmaker's ability to balance color and form. The Garden quilts often were embellished with crewel embroidery worked in wools or silk floss, and crewel work also was sometimes used to form the entire design. The beautiful quilt pictured in Fig. 4-34 is a more modern version of a "Garden" pattern. It displays a central medallion of flower-filled baskets, balanced by a single flower basket motif along each of the four sides.

Making an appliqué quilt with an overall design was an awkward task because it necessitated beginning the work in the middle of the quilt and proceeding outward while holding a lapful of fabric. Many quiltmakers preferred to make their appliqué designs in block units that later were set together to form the quilt top. The "Tulip" appliqué quilt shown in Fig. 4-35 was made this way, the blocks set together with alternating plain blocks and a pieced latticework to form the total design. The same quiltmaker designed both the tulip and the flower basket appliqué quilts and also pieced the "World's Puzzle" quilt (Fig. 4-28), all three of which are outstanding examples of fine quiltmaking.

Although many of the old appliqué quilts were the result of the individual quiltmaker's fancies, there are four basic appliqué block designs that reappear again and again on old quilt tops. One is the traditional "rose" design and its variations, and another is the "garden wreath" of the quiltmaker's favorite flowers. E in the color section illustrates a well-known variation of the traditional rose design, named

FIG. 4–34. (*above left*) "Garden Basket" appliqué quilt.

FIG. 4–35. (*above right*) "Tulip" appliqué quilt.

the "Rose of Sharon." A more complex version, pictured in B in the color section, combines both the fundamental rose and wreath designs in large wreaths of roses and tulips. The other two basic appliqué block designs are the "leaf cluster," often composed of oak leaves, and the "princess feather," reminiscent of the eighteenth-century plumed headdresses worn at Court presentations.

Appliqué quilts often were finished off with an elaborate appliquéd border that carried through the main motif. A very fine example is the border of the "Rose of Sharon" quilt in B in the color section. The choice of a border for a quilt design was again a matter of the quiltmaker's personal taste and eye for design. The pieced designs of the "Flower Garden" (Fig. 4-5) and the "Double Wedding Ring" (Fig. 4-36) finish out in scalloped edges and do not require a border. On the other hand, the appliquéd "Dolls" quilt (Fig. 4-37) and the "Dresden Plate" (Fig. 4-38) were made with pieced borders creating scalloped edges to add detail to the overall design. Some pieced designs like the "World's Puzzle" quilt (Fig. 4-28) and the variation of the

FIG. 4–36. (*upper left*) "Double Wedding Ring" pieced quilt.

FIG. 4–37. (*above*) "Dolls" or "Sunbonnet Sue" appliqué quilt.

FIG. 4–38. (*left*) "Dresden Plate" pieced quilt.

"World Without End" quilt (Fig. 4-33) are most effectively finished off with a simple framework border. The "Star of Hope" quilt (G in the color section) could have been made with a framework border, but by using the angular "Saw Tooth" border, the quiltmaker further emphasized the pointed stars in the pattern. The choice of border and the way in which the overall design is set together are part of the unique quality of each patchwork quilt.

American patchwork quilts, in contrast to European quilting, are distinctive in that the quilting pattern is considered to be an integral part of the overall design. Traditional quiltmakers take great care to choose a quilting pattern that complements the design of the pieced or appliquéd top. For instance, the lines of a geometric pieced pattern, such as the "Baseball" pattern that is being quilted in Fig. 4-39, are emphasized by outline stitching. Plain blocks in a pattern are decorated by "fancy" quilting motifs such as the design that the quilters shown in Fig. 4-40 are stitching on the white blocks of the "Single Irish Chain" pattern. Instead of outline-stitching the print squares in the "Irish Chain," the quilters have chosen to stitch a small circle on each of the plain blocks, which is an interesting contrast from a design standpoint and also carries through the circular floral motif. The reverse side of the "Improved Nine-Patch" quilt in Fig. 4-41 clearly shows how the quiltmaker has emphasized the geometric lines of the design by not only outline-stitching the pieced pattern but by quilting a complementary geometric design on the plain blocks that set the pattern together. Thus the quilting not only serves to emphasize the pieced pattern but creates a handsome design in its own right on the reverse side of the quilt.

As a general rule, American quiltmakers used "fancy" quilting motifs only to fill in the open spaces in the overall design. Among the "fancy" motifs found on old quilts are many varieties of floral bouquets and wreaths, the pineapple, the spider web, oak leaves, the weeping willow, stars, and cornucopias. Both the American eagle and the dove of peace were popular old designs, and of course hearts were a favorite motif for a bridal quilt. The "Princess Feather" (Figs. 4-42 and 4-43), which also was used as an appliqué design, was one of the most popular quilting motifs, either as a block design to decorate open spaces in the overall pattern or as a "running" border design. The "Garden" appliqué quilt in Fig. 4-34 has a princess

FIG. 4–39. (*upper left*) Quilter emphasizing geometric "Baseball" pattern by outline quilting.

FIG. 4–40. (*above*) "Fancy" floral quilting motif decorates plain blocks in a "Single Irish Chain" quilt.

FIG. 4–41. (*left*) Reverse side of "Improved Nine-Patch" pieced quilt showing quilting design.

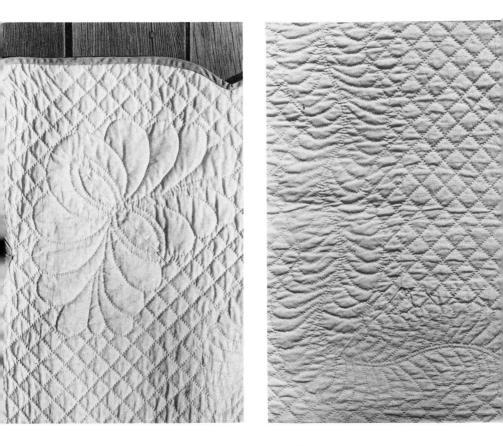

FIGS. 4–42 & 4–43. Details of "Princess Feather" quilting designs.

feather border around the central appliquéd medallion and a feather motif quilted in each of the corners of the quilt. The "Tulip" appliqué quilt in Fig. 4-35 has a princess feather wreath quilted on each of the plain blocks of the design. Other quilting designs used for "running" borders are the "Cable," which is the border for the "Crow's Foot" quilt in Fig. 5-3, and the "Tea Cup" (Fig. 4-44), the "Ocean Wave" (Fig. 4-45), the "Interlocked Diamonds" (Fig. 4-46), and the "Egg and Dart" (Fig. 4-47).

A second general rule of American quiltmakers was that an elaborately pieced or appliquéd design called for an overall background of "plain" quilting in contrast with fancy quilting filling in the open spaces of the design. Thus, both the "Garden" and "Tulip" appliqué quilts are quilted in an overall pattern of diamonds, in addition to the fancy princess feather quilting. Besides diamonds (Fig. 4-48), traditional "plain" quilting patterns included single, double, or triple

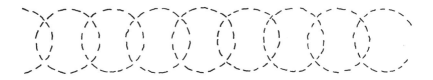

FIG. 4–44. "Tea Cup."

FIG. 4–45. "Ocean Wave."

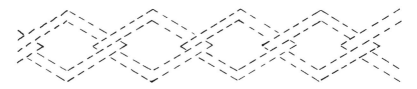

FIG. 4–46. "Interlocked Diamonds."

FIG. 4–47. (*above*) "Egg and Dart."

FIG. 4–48 (*below*) "Diamond."

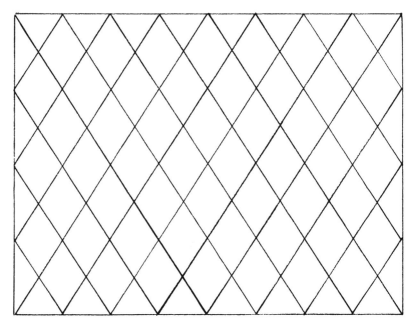

rows of diagonal lines (Fig. 4-49), or crossbars, and on a few very old quilts an overall pattern called the "Clam Shell" (Fig. 4-50)

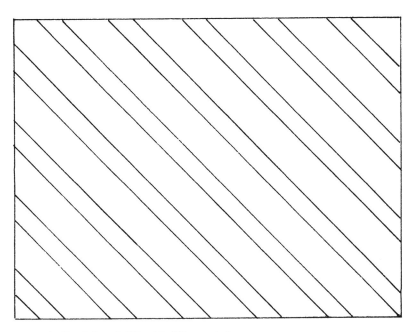

FIG. 4–49. (*above*) "Double Diagonals."

FIG. 4–50. (*below*) "Clam Shell."

also was used as a "plain" quilting design. The "Rose of Sharon" quilt (B in the color section) is closely quilted in double rows of diagonal lines with princess feather wreaths between each of the appliquéd rose and tulip wreaths. The "Saw Tooth" quilt in Fig. 4-51 is quilted in an overall pattern of diagonal lines with double rows of diagonal lines in the pattern blocks, princess feather wreaths in the plain blocks, and a princess feather running border.

Intricate quilting is a clue to the relative age of a quilt. Today even experienced quilters seldom attempt to do the kind of quilting their grandmothers did—minute stitches as regular as though they had been stitched by a machine, rows of stitching so close together that it is difficult to distinguish one row from the next, and every square inch of the quilt covered with the quilting design. The apex of the art of quilting was achieved in the all-white "plain" quilts that displayed the quiltmaker's proficiency at needlework, and, incidentally, her infinite patience. The design of these quilts was formed entirely by the quilting stitches that typically formed a central medallion surrounded by a series of borders. Sometimes the medallion was stuffed underneath with cotton to create a relief effect, or the background quilting around the medallion was stitched so close together that it produced a textured surface known as "blister" quilting.

The elaborately quilted "plain" quilts are highly prized by farm women who carry on the tradition of quiltmaking, but these days they are being made in contemporary colors, such as avocado or gold, instead of the traditional all-white. Many of the quilts made by the Mennonite churchwomen for the annual quilt auctions are "plain" quilts or embroidered designs like the cross-stitched "Double Wedding Ring" quilt in Fig. 4-52. Today's quiltmakers take advantage of the puffy quality of the synthetic fiberfill to create a three-dimensional effect in the beautifully stitched quilting designs.

Another quilting technique used to create a relief effect was the corded or "trapunto" quilting. A piece of loosely woven fabric was basted to the underside of the quilt top, then outline-stitched on the back side in a design that was corded by forcing wool yarn in between the lines of the stitching to form a raised design on the quilt top. Trapunto quilting was widely used in England and on the Continent

 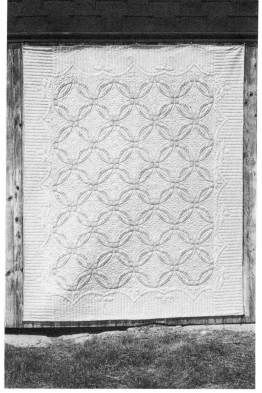

FIG. 4–51. (*above left*) Reverse side of "Saw Tooth" quilt, showing quilting designs.

FIG. 4–52. (*above right*) Cross-stitched "Double Wedding Ring" quilt.

during the seventeenth and eighteenth centuries to decorate petticoats, caps, and other garments, as well as to make counterpanes of exquisite beauty. Because it was meant to be decorative rather than functional, trapunto quilting was often done on delicate silks, satins, and velvets, and no batting was used between the layers of fabric. Trapunto is still used for decorative details on women's clothing, and is a technique that lends itself to contemporary quilting experiments in creating three-dimensional designs and sculptured fabric objects.

CHAPTER V
Quilt Names and Superstitions

The names of old patchwork quilt patterns—"Drunkard's Path," "Wandering Foot," "Fifty-four Forty or Fight," to mention only a few —are as vigorous as the designs themselves. Unlike many other hand-crafts, quilts always were given a name of their own. Provocative clues to the life experiences and concerns of generations of American quiltmakers lie in the names they chose for their patchwork quilts, for quite often the name of a specific pattern was changed by the individual quiltmaker. The many superstitions concerning quilts also indicate that they were not merely handcrafts but objects of some symbolic importance in the lives of the women and men who made them.

Among the superstitions regarding the bridal quilt was the belief that terrible consequences might result if a young lady become too anxious about her future and started to make her bridal quilt before she was spoken for. Also, it was considered bad luck to use hearts as part of a patchwork or quilting design unless the quiltmaker was officially engaged. The favorite pattern for a bridal quilt was the "Rose of Sharon," the most famous of all the old appliqué rose patterns. The name "Rose of Sharon" is taken from the poetic de-scription of love between a woman and a man contained in the Song of Solomon: "I am the rose of Sharon, and the lily of the valleys. As the lily among thorns, so is my love among the daughters.

As the apple tree among the trees of the wood, so is my beloved among the sons. I sat down under his shadow with great delight, and his fruit was sweet to my taste. He brought me to the banqueting house, and his banner over me was love. Stay me with flagons, comfort me with apples: for I am sick of love." The Victorians did not approve of such a plainspoken description of the pleasures of love even though it was part of the Bible, and young maidens were forbidden to read Solomon's songs, but for generations they continued to make the traditional "Rose of Sharon" for their bridal quilts.

However, no young lady in her right senses ever considered making the old pattern known as the "Wandering Foot" as one of her trousseau quilts, for superstition held that any male who slept under a quilt of this pattern would develop a restlessness to leave his familiar surroundings and see the world, possibly never to return home again. At some unknown point in the history of American quiltmaking, the "Wandering Foot" pattern was renamed "Turkey Tracks," which evidently eliminated the superstition, and from then on quilts of this pattern were considered safe to use on the beds of boys and young men of marriageable age.

Some old quilts display a small patch of color that is violently at odds with the overall color scheme, or have an error in one part of the design, like the upside-down basket in one row of the quilt pattern in D in the color section. Such mistakes were deliberately made to ensure good luck following the Near Eastern belief that perfection imitates the Deity and therefore is both presumptuous and unlucky. Another superstition in quiltmaking lore was concerned with the design at the corners of the quilt. If a running border design was used, it had to be carefully planned to turn the corner without a break, for a broken design foretold that the quiltmaker's life would be cut short by disaster.

Surprising to contemporary viewers, the swastika is a good-luck symbol that is frequently seen in old quilt designs. It is a graphic symbol found in almost every ancient and primitive cult all over the world. It appears in both North American Indian art and traditional Pennsylvania-German folk art where it is often used as a decoration although outsiders have misinterpreted it as being a "hex" against witches. As a symbol the swastika represents the movement and power of the sun as related to the poles and the four cardinal directions, but it has lost its ancient significance and would be of little interest in the modern world had not Hitler used it for the flag of the Nazi Third Reich on the advice of his occultists. The swastika design used on old quilts was variously named "Crazy Ann," "Follow the Leader," "Twist and Turn," and the "Fly Foot," the latter name probably being derived from the "fylfot fret," a decorative detail based on the swastika shape and widely used in colonial architecture.

Another good-luck symbol was the pineapple motif, a traditional sign of domestic hospitality. Pineapples first grew in tropical America and were brought back to Europe by the Spanish after their explorations in South America. For many years they were cultivated in the kitchen gardens of Europe and that they were well known to the early American colonists is evident from the frequent appearance of carved pineapple designs in colonial furniture. The pineapple was one of the favorite quilting designs and also was used as a design for appliqué quilts.

Fruits, vegetables and flowers, trees and leaves, the sun and the stars, birds and animals, and even insects, all the works of nature, provided inspiration for old patchwork designs. The pomegranate, an ancient symbol of fecundity, is one of the more unusual appliquéd fruit designs, but it was a common motif in the prized hand-painted India chintzes. The wild grapevines that the early American colonists found growing in the dense forests provided the basis for a popular quilt border design known as the "Trailing Vine" and bunches of grapes and vines often were used in appliquéd garden quilt designs. The "Melon Patch" is immortalized in an old pieced pattern, as are "Corn and Beans," a pattern dating from the days when pole beans were planted between the rows of sweet corn in the kitchen garden. A popular appliqué design, the "Love Apple," was actually named after the tomato. Like the pineapple, the tomato is native to tropical America and was brought back to Europe as one of the curiosities of the New World. Although considered to be inedible, both the red and yellow varieties of the tomato plant were grown in flower gardens for their ornamental value. It was thought that the tomato stimulated love, hence the name love apple, and the origin of the old quilt design, which usually was made up in red and yellow with realistic tomato leaves. The tomato did not become a popular food until after the Civil War period and even then it was first served as a rich preserve rather than a vegetable. Flowers abound in old quilt patterns, too, and probably every flower native to North America, including the cactus, has been the inspiration of a quilt pattern at some time in the history of American quiltmaking.

"Hens and Chickens" was among the quilt patterns named for birds, as well as the "Swallow" and "Dove in the Window," the latter a reminder of the specially constructed windows up near the rafters of old barns where the pet pigeons could fly in to roost. The wily old fox who raided the barnyard fowls lives on in the pieced pattern "Fox and Geese." The butterfly, the honeybee, and the shoofly all have quilt patterns named after them, and there is even an intricate pieced pattern named the "Snail Trail." Another motif taken from the India chintzes was the peacock. In Christian art, the peacock is a symbol of immortality and of the incorruptible soul, and his beautiful plumage was frequently used as a motif in traditional Pennsylvania-German folk art. Among the many quilt patterns based on the sun and on the stars are the "Sunburst" quilt in Fig. 5-1 and the "Oklahoma Star" in Fig. 5-2.

Often the name of a particular pattern would vary from one region of the country to another. The lily pattern, based on the old "Star of LeMoyne," has eight different names according to the variety of lily common in the locale where the quiltmaker lived. In northern New England, it was called the "Wood Lily"; in southern New England, the "Meadow Lily"; and in Pennsylvania, the "Tiger Lily." Throughout the South, it was known as the "North Carolina Lily," except in Kentucky and Tennessee where it was the "Mountain Lily." Quiltmakers living in Ohio, Indiana, and Illinois named their lily-pattern quilts the "Fire Lily" after a common weed that bears five red bell flowers. West of the Mississippi, the lily pattern was known as the "Prairie Lily" and beyond the Great Divide it was called the "Mariposa Lily."

In renaming an old quilt pattern, the quiltmaker naturally chose

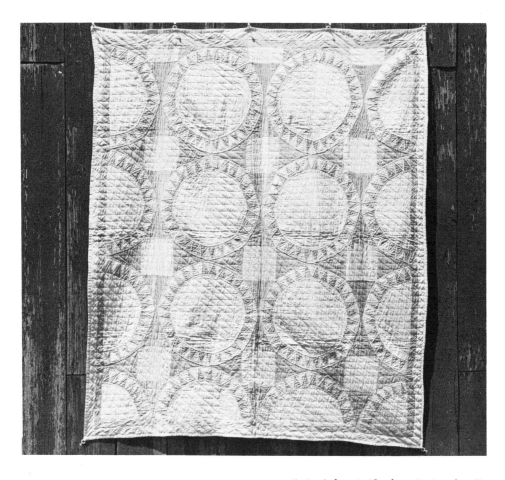

FIG. 5–1. (*above*) "Sunburst" pieced quilt.

FIG. 5–2. (*left*) "Oklahoma Star" pieced quilt.

a name with familiar associations. The quilt shown in Fig. 5-3 is known as the "Crow's Foot" in central Illinois where the pesky crows are such a nuisance in the cornfields, but it is the same as a very old pattern called the "Bear's Paw" in the eastern part of the United States. To other quiltmakers the pattern had other associations: on Long Island, it became the "Duck's Foot in the Mud" in honor of the famous ducklings that have been bred there since the time of the early Dutch settlers; and among the Philadelphia Quakers, it became the "Hand of Friendship."

Many names of old patchwork patterns are dynamic expressions of American history. The "Log Cabin" pattern in Fig. 5-4 commemorates the countless women like Christiana Tillson and Rebecca Burlend and great-great-grandmother Barbara Reeser who made a crude log cabin in the wilderness into a home. No quilt design could be more authentically American than the "Pine Tree," the prerevolutionary symbol of the original American colonies. As far back as 1652, coinage minted in the Massachusetts colony was struck with the image of a pine tree, and later the pine tree flag came to symbolize the American colonies' fight for freedom against British oppression. The bald eagle, the emblem of the Great Seal of the United States of America, often appeared on quilts either as an appliqué design or as a quilting pattern. At any threat to the Union such as the War of 1812 or the Mexican War in 1846, quiltmakers expressed their patriotic sentiments by making quilts displaying the American Eagle.

The old pieced pattern "Fifty-four Forty or Fight" was taken from a popular slogan in the 1830s and 1840s during the boundary dispute between the United States and Great Britain over the Oregon territory. Dissension over slavery caused some quiltmakers to change the names of several old patterns to express their own feelings: the prerevolutionary pieced pattern "Jacob's Ladder" became the "Underground Railroad" in parts of the North, and "Job's Tears," another traditional pieced pattern, was renamed the "Slave Chain." Northern quiltmakers also revived the American Eagle as a quilt design during the Civil War era to signify their support of the Union.

Although women did not achieve the right to vote until 1920, that they took a keen interest in the political issues of their day is

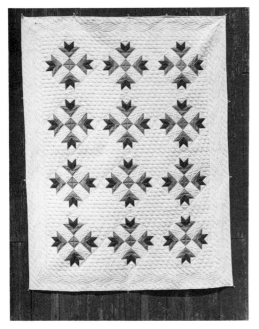

FIG. 5–3. (*left*) "Crow's Foot" pieced quilt.

FIG. 5–4. (*below*) "Log Cabin" pieced quilt.

exemplified by the names they gave to some of their patchwork patterns. The "Whig Rose," an appliqué pattern based on the basic rose design, was so popular among quiltmakers that the Democrats claimed it too and the controversy was never settled as to which political party the design originally belonged. The pattern "Tippecanoe and Tyler Too" came from the campaign slogan of William Henry Harrison, nicknamed "Old Tippecanoe," who was elected President in 1840 with John Tyler as Vice-President. Stephen A. Douglas, who defeated Abraham Lincoln in 1858 for the United States senatorial seat from Illinois, may be an almost forgotten figure in political history, but there is an old quilt pattern bearing his nickname, the "Little Giant." Not only Presidents and politicians were honored by old quilt patterns—Barbara Frietchie, Martha Washington, and Dolley Madison all have a "star" named after them, too.

Religious faith was a vital force in pioneer American life, and many old quilt patterns bear Biblical names. The "Star of Bethlehem" has already been mentioned as one of the popular pieced patterns, and there were also "King David's Crown," the "Star and Cross," "Golgotha," and "Palm Leaves Hosanna," to name only a few. "Delectable Mountains," the name of an overall pieced design, was taken from John Bunyan's *Pilgrim's Progress*, and the quilt in Fig. 4-33 is an adaptation of an old pattern known as "World Without End," a phrase from the Book of Common Prayer. The devil wasn't forgotten by quiltmakers either; interestingly enough, another old name for the "Fly Foot" or swastika pattern was the "Devil's Puzzle."

The unusual Biblical quilt in Fig. 5-5 is composed of twenty-four embroidered scenes from the Old Testament with one scene showing a man in stocks and labeled "Colonial Justice." The central Illinois quiltmaker who made this quilt for one of her grandsons passed away thirty years ago and no one in the family now remembers if Grandma designed the quilt herself or copied the scenes from something she had seen in a newspaper or farm magazine. Until around the time of the Second World War, many of the midwestern newspapers routinely published pieced and appliquéd quilt patterns and quilting designs, and some of the farm magazines still provide publications on quilts and other needlecraft. The scenes in this charming

FIG. 5–5. "Biblical" embroidered quilt.

quilt are outline-stitched in black on white blocks and include a scroll bearing the words "God," "Heaven," "Earth," "Air," "Water," and "Life"; Adam with a lion and a lamb; Eve with the serpent and the apple; the Altar of Sacrifice; the Tower of Babel; Abraham and Isaac; the Pillar of Salt; Joseph sold into Egypt; Moses; the Rock of Living Water; the Spies with the grapes; Solomon the Wise Judge; Jacob's Dream; the Ark; David and Jonathan; Samuel and Saul; Rebecca at the Well; Sampson and the lion; Elijah and the ravens; Ruth the gleaner; the Fall of Jericho; Colonial Justice; David and Goliath; Daniel in the Lions' Den; and Gideon and the fleece.

Even the very ordinary objects of everyday life provided American quiltmakers with inspiration for patchwork patterns. The "Churn Dash" is a reminder of the days when cream had to be hand-churned into butter, and the "Reel" was named after the wooden reel used to wind wool into skeins for spinning. Masculine occupations were represented among old patchwork patterns by the "Anvil," the "Dusty

Miller," and "Chips and Whetstones," while the "Spool" brings to mind great-grandmother's never-ending task of sewing and mending clothing for her family. The "Dresden Plate" (Fig. 4-38) and the "Pickle Dish" (Fig. 7-1) resemble the prized china and cut-glass dishes that graced the table for company dinners. Feminine apparel also served as a source of patchwork designs—the "Fan," a very old pattern; the "Sunbonnet," another name for the "Dolls" quilt in Fig. 4-37; and "Tangled Garters," an intriguing name for a quilt.

From the "Rose of Sharon" to the "Double Wedding Ring," "Baby's Blocks," and finally "Grandmother's Flower Garden," old patchwork quilt patterns span a lifetime of experiences.

CHAPTER VI
Quilt Fabrics and Dyes

Determined to make colorful quilts from the drab homespun, often the only new cloth available in pioneer days, the ingenious quilt-makers dyed the plain fabric with the natural dyes at their disposal. Until 1856, when an English chemist accidentally produced the first synthetic dye, the only dyes available for either home or commercial use were the natural vegetable, mineral, and animal dyes. The indigo plant from the East Indies yielded a rich blue that was commonly used to dye homespun linsey-woolsey, and the roots of the madder plant grown in the Levant and Italy produced both brown dyes and the brilliant Turkey red beloved by quiltmakers. Black came from logwood, a tree native to tropical America, and yellow from the wood of the fustic tree of the West Indies. Another blue dye was extracted from the leaves of the woad plant, native to England where the inhabitants of the island used it many centuries ago to stain their bodies. One of the few animal dyes was a bright carmine obtained from the cochineal insects of Mexico and South America. Block tin from the mines of Cornwall, when melted and dissolved in aqua fortis, was used in dyeing cloth crimson and yellow, and other mineral dyes produced manganese brown, Prussian blue, chrome yellow, and iron buff.

In addition to all the dyestuffs imported to America and readily available at chemists and grocery stores, the pioneers found any number of native vegetable dyes such as the black walnut shells that great-great-grandmother Reeser used to dye yarn for stockings a practical greenish-brown color. The bark of maple, white oak, walnut, butternut, and chestnut trees all yield dyes, as do sumac berries, pokeberries, nutgalls, sedge grass, and even the flowers of the black-eyed Susan. Several different colors could be produced from the same dye by using a "mordant" such as alum or copperas, substances that attracted and held the dye permanently in the fabric.

Old dye recipes are fascinating to read, but experience in using them is obviously a necessary ingredient, for the instructions sound like those of an experienced cook who doesn't need to rely on measurements—take a handful of this and a pinch of that and just boil it until it gets done. Among the recipes published in *Godey's Lady's Book* for July to December, 1855, is one for brown dye: "A decoction of oak bark dyes wool a fast brown of various shades according to the quantity employed; an infusion of walnut peels will also dye brown. The wool should be previously dipped in a solution of alum and water, which brightens the color." "For blue dye; boil in a bath of logwood to which a small quantity of blue vitriol has been added, using the alum bath as in the other cases." For black dye, "Logwood and green copperas are commonly used, but the color is improved by first boiling the article in a decoction of galls and alderbark. If previously dyed blue or brown, by means of walnut-peels, it will be still better." A great many trial-and-error experiments would have to take place for a novice at dyeing to successfully follow these recipes, but in the pioneer days, dye recipes were passed down from mother to daughter along with all the other knowledge of the household arts.

Both red and blue appear frequently in old quilts because Turkey red and indigo blue were the most colorfast of all the vegetable dyes. The colors did not run or fade despite repeated washings. Red and white, or blue and white, were the traditional combination for many of the overall pieced patterns like the "Drunkard's Path" and all its variations. It is unfortunate that the quiltmaker who made the "World's Puzzle" quilt in Fig. 4-28, the name she gave to the traditional "Drunkard's Path" pattern, did not have available the old vegetable-dyed Turkey-red cotton because the poorly dyed red cotton in this quilt has run into the white of the pattern. The quilt was made during World War I when the good synthetic dyes, which were largely produced by Germany, were in short supply. Since then, the United States has become the world's leading manufacturer of synthetic dyes, most of them products distilled from coal tar, which are much more colorfast than the old natural dyes.

Green also appears in old quilts but it often is a bluish-green or yellowish-green. There was no natural dye that produced a solid green and the color had to be obtained by a combination of blue and yellow dyes. In making green printed cottons, indigo blue had to be hand-printed or sometimes hand-painted on yellow, or vice versa, to obtain the green print. Another method used to print greens, and cotton prints in general, was the "resist" process known as "batik" in Java where it has been used for centuries. A "resist" is a substance such as wax or clay that is applied to either the design or the background before the fabric is dipped into the dye. The parts of the fabric that have been covered with the resist do not absorb the dye. Thus it is possible, for example, to print a blue figure on a green background by first dyeing the fabric blue, then covering the blue design with wax and dipping the fabric in yellow dye to obtain the green background.

Both the ancient techniques of wax-resist and of tie-dyeing, wherein parts of the fabric are tightly bunched together and tied with string to protect them from the successive dye baths, have become very popular again in recent years to create contemporary fabric designs. Although few of us have tree bark or wild berries readily at hand to experiment with the old natural dye recipes, we do have available the peelings from carrots and red beets, and onion skins, all of which produce lovely soft colors when boiled for about an hour, depending on the desired intensity of the color, in a big pot of water with a tablespoon of vinegar added to set the color. But anyone who has tried home-dyeing, using either natural or synthetic dyes, quickly discovers that it is a messy, awkward task to dye even a yard of fabric so that the color is even, and one marvels at the persistence of the pioneer housewives who somehow managed to dye whole bolts of cloth in a twenty-gallon copper boiler hung over an open fire. Persist they did, for the feminine love of bright colors is not to be denied.

The appearance of quilts was of course greatly influenced by the dressmaker fashions over the years. As has been mentioned, the India chintzes imported into Europe from the mid-1600s were exceedingly popular not only as dress materials but also as cut-out motifs for appliquéd quilt designs. The manufacture of hand-printed cottons quickly developed in Europe in response to this popularity, but for a while, due to pressure from the woolen and linen manufacturers, the governments of both England and France forbade by law the use of hand-painted or -printed cottons, whether imported or manufactured at home. Mere laws, however, were not enough to deter females from wearing brightly colored dresses, and a brisk trade in illegal cotton prints was carried on until the laws were finally repealed. As a compensation to the woolen and linen industries, a tax was imposed on all cottons manufactured in England, which was doubled on the cottons imported to the American colonies. This tax was bitterly resented in the colonies and was one of the factors contributing to the general discontent that fostered the American Revolution. To circumvent the tax on manufactured cotton goods, almost every household in the American colonies had a loom. A license was required and a tax was imposed on it, too, but despite this it was still cheaper to spin and weave all the cloth needed for household use. Aside from the housewives' own efforts to dye their homespun, there was a flourishing trade conducted by professional dyers who also undertook to decorate homespun in the manner of the prized cotton prints by hand-painting or by hand-printing using the wood block or copperplate methods.

The weaving of woolens and of linens and of the combination known as linsey-woolsey flourished as a home industry in the American colonies despite the British restrictions, but cotton was never one of the homespun industries. After the Revolution it was difficult to get the cotton industry started in America because England jealously guarded the patent rights to all the mechanical inventions—the spinning jenny, the fly shuttle, the spinning frame, and the power loom—which had industrialized cotton manufacturing. However, skilled English workmen, in particular Samuel Slater, memorized the plans of the English inventions and brought them to America where, by the early 1790s, Slater's cotton mill in Pawtucket, Rhode Island, was in full operation. Only a few years later, in 1814, the Lowell cotton factory in Waltham, Massachusetts, was the first mill in the world to combine all the operations of taking raw cotton and making it into finished cloth under one roof.

Although at various times in the history of American quiltmaking many fabrics other than cotton were used out of necessity, quiltmakers have preferred to make their quilts from the printed cottons known to our grandmothers as calico. Two major exceptions were the Southern appliqué quilts and the Victorian crazy quilts, both of which were made for their decorative value rather than functional use. Otherwise, for three hundred years the cotton prints, washable, color-fast, and soft yet durable, have been and still are today the preferred fabrics for patchwork quilts.

The brilliant color combinations such as red with various shades of purple that predominated in the dress materials and also in the quilts of the revolutionary period are startling to contemporary viewers accustomed to thinking that all our colonial ancestors dressed in the dark colors of the Puritans. With the introduction of manganese bronze as a commercial dye in the early 1800s, brown printed in blue, green, red, or purple was immediately popular as dress material, and brown prints then dominated the quilts, too. Later, during the Mexican War period, the fashionable dress materials were lavender and gray delicately figured in black or white, but the bright reds and greens figured in yellow or black that turned up in quilts were widely used for curtain and upholstery fabrics. After the Civil War when cotton prints became very expensive, brown again became a favorite color for dresses, and the variety of prints in the "Century" quilt in E in the color section is typical of that period. This "Century" quilt and the "Nine-Patch" quilt in Fig. 6-1 were both made sometime before 1877. The pieced design of the "Nine-Patch" is made of a red cotton printed with black, and the background is white cotton finely crosshatched in black, characteristic of the printed cottons available before the Civil War. However, the ages of the fabrics used are not an accurate guide to the actual age

FIG. 6–1. "Nine-Patch" pieced quilt.

of a quilt because quiltmakers often had to accumulate scraps for years until they had enough of a particular color to carry out a planned design.

CHAPTER VII
Three Generations
of Quiltmakers

A treasury of quilts, old and new, pieced and appliquéd, is to be found, not in a museum, but in a tiny town southeast of Kansas City, Missouri, the home of seventy-five-year-old Aunt Olive Fischer. Aunt Olive, who herself is a prolific quiltmaker, has a collection of quilts made by her grandmother, aunt, and mother, the oldest of which dates back to 1852. Not only has Aunt Olive made so many quilts that she has lost count of them all, she also is accomplished at crocheting, tatting, and knitting. The drawers and trunks of her home are filled with examples of her fine needlework, and no one knows how many quilts and crocheted table linens she has given away as gifts or made as custom orders over the years.

The highlight of Aunt Olive's quilt collection is the exquisite "Rose of Sharon" quilt pictured in B in the color section, which was made by her paternal grandmother, Catherine McCulloh, when she was sixteen years old. Quite likely Grandmother Catherine made it as her bridal quilt, for it has been carefully preserved throughout three lifetimes and is in perfect condition today. The roses and tulips in the nine appliquéd wreaths are made of Turkey-red cotton, and the green print used for the leaves has a yellowish-green fleur-de-lis pattern. Some of the red roses have gold centers, which were appliquéd by the technique known as "in-lay." The red rose was laid on the background and stitched down, then a circle was cut in the center of the rose to expose the gold patch that had been placed underneath and the raw edges of the circle were buttonhole-stitched down. The beautiful appliqué work on this quilt, in particular the unusual appliquéd border design, and the fine quilting, indicate that it was indeed a "labor of love."

Aunt Olive has another lovely "Rose of Sharon" quilt, the one shown in E in the color section, which was made by her mother's oldest sister, Sarah Elizabeth Brewbaker. The exact age of this quilt is not certain, but Aunt Sarah Elizabeth, who was born in 1850, died at the age of twenty-seven of tuberculosis, so the quilt had to be made before 1877. This quilt is especially interesting because the roses are a soft brown, dyed with onion skins. The green leaves probably also were home-dyed, as the fabric of both the roses and the leaves appears to have been the same unbleached muslin used for the background of the quilt. Aunt Olive recalls her mother saying that the family used to make all their household linens from the big rolls of unbleached muslin, two feet in width, which her father purchased on trips to town. Although the textile industry was well established in America by 1840, cotton prints became very expensive after the Civil War and this thrifty Scotch-Irish family evidently made do with plain unbleached muslin. Nevertheless, Aunt Sarah Elizabeth was able to make a lovely quilt by following the example of generations of resourceful housewives and dyeing the plain muslin with natural dyes.

The "Century" quilt in E in the color section and the "Nine-Patch" quilt in Fig. 6-1 also were made by Aunt Sarah Elizabeth, and later the three quilts were passed on to her younger sister, Laura. When she married in 1893, Laura Brewbaker Fritz moved from her family home in Mercersburg, Pennsylvania, to Index, Missouri, taking with her Sarah Elizabeth's three quilts and the "Rose of Sharon" quilt that had been made by her husband's mother, Catherine McCulloh Fritz. An invalid during the last twenty years of her life, Laura Fritz kept herself occupied by making quilts, among them the "Star of Hope" (G of the color section), the "Quilt of a Thousand Prints" (D of the color section), and the incredible "Dime-Size Flower Garden" (Fig. 4-6). All the quilts made by the Brewbaker sisters,

FIG. 7–1. "Pickle Dish" pieced quilt.

Sarah Elizabeth and Laura, display a skill at fine needlework and quilting second to none in the annals of quiltmaking history, and this family tradition is being ably carried on by Laura's only daughter, Olive Fritz Fischer.

In G of the color section, Aunt Olive is shown sitting in the swing on her front porch with a "Flower Garden" quilt that she had just finished quilting a few days before. Some of the many other quilts she has made are the "Oklahoma Star" (Fig. 5-2), the "Cottage Tulip" (Fig. 4-22), the "Pickle Dish" (Fig. 7-1), and the "Rock Garden" (G in the color section). In addition to all of her finished quilts, Aunt Olive has at least eight pieced and appliquéd quilt tops all ready for quilting during the winter when she won't be busy gardening and will have time to work on them. An energetic woman all her life, Aunt Olive is plagued with health problems and can't get around as easily now, but her fingers are always busy with all the various quilting and needlework projects that she has in mind to do, enough to keep her occupied for another lifetime.

CHAPTER VIII
How-to-Do-It

Making a patchwork quilt can be easy, and here is how you go about it. Unlike many other crafts, quiltmaking does not require investing in expensive equipment. You probably already have most of the items you will need—a pair of sharp scissors, a short sewing needle and white thread, and a ruler, chalk, and cardboard for making the pattern. It isn't even necessary to buy a bulky quilting frame that you may not have space for in your home. Using a large embroidery hoop to hold the three layers of the quilt taut is more convenient when you are learning to quilt than permanently attaching the quilt to a frame. And the embroidery hoop can be easily stored away when not in use.

Also, you don't need to be an accomplished seamstress to make a patchwork quilt. The simple in-and-out running stitch that everyone automatically uses to stitch together two pieces of cloth is used in sewing the patches in a pieced quilt. An appliqué quilt is made by sewing down the appliqué pieces with the same stitch used in hemming a skirt. Quilting consists of stitching through the three layers of the quilt using the basic running stitch. Sewing a quilt is that simple.

What is essential in quiltmaking is the desire to finish a quilt that you can proudly display, which means that you will take the time to follow the pattern exactly. It is important that you carefully cut the pieces of the pattern, using a "template" or cardboard pattern as a guide, so that all the pieces are the same size. If you also are careful to maintain the same amount of seam allowance in sewing together the pieces of the pattern, the overall design will be uniform and the surface of the quilt will lay smoothly. Accuracy in the beginning stages of making your quilt will save needless frustration later on.

Planning your quilt

The first consideration is to choose a pattern and plan the overall design of your quilt. Do you prefer the appliquéd or the pieced patterns? Do you want to make a traditional pattern or dream up your own? And how big does the quilt need to be for the bed that you intend to use it on?

Beginning quiltmakers often prefer to start with an appliquéd rather than a pieced quilt because there is greater freedom of design. Once you have mastered the simple technique of appliqué, you will be able to make any design that you choose. Also, if you are proficient at using a sewing machine, you can easily do appliqué work with the zigzag attachment. Although many of the pieced patterns can be made on the sewing machine too, it is more difficult to handle the tiny patches when sewing by machine, and you will need to experiment for yourself with the particular pattern you wish to make.

The bold but relatively simple overall pieced patterns, such as the "Log Cabin" (Fig. 5-4) and all its variations, are recommended for a beginning quiltmaker. The crazy quilt and all the one-patch patterns also are easy to sew, and other uncomplicated pieced patterns have been mentioned in the design section. In general, patterns formed by diamond patches or by curved patches are frustrating for a novice quiltmaker because of the difficulty in sewing the patches together smoothly. If you aren't sure how difficult a particular pattern might be to make, try sewing one block unit out of scraps before you go to the expense of buying the fabric for your quilt.

It is important to plan the overall design of your quilt so that you can estimate how much fabric you will need. If you intend to use your quilt as a bedspread, it must be made to fit the bed on which it will be used. The following chart gives the measurements for standard size mattresses, but it is a good idea to check the measurements of your bed, particularly the height of the bed from the floor to the top of the mattress. In the chart, 20 inches has been used as the standard bed height, and another 20 inches has been added for the length necessary to go over the pillows.

Bed	Mattress Measurements	Bedspread
Twin	39″ x 78″	79″ x 118″
Double	54″ x 78″	94″ x 118″
Queen	60″ x 78″	100″ x 118″
King	72″ x 84″	112″ x 124″

If you have a queen- or king-size bed and despair at the thought of making a quilt large enough to completely cover it, consider using a dust ruffle with a coverlet that goes over the pillows and just drapes over the sides of the bed. Depending on the pattern you choose, there are several ways that the size of a quilt can be enlarged with a minimum of sewing, either by adding on borders or by setting the pattern blocks together with plain blocks. Also, the proportions of some patterns can be enlarged. For instance, the hexagon-shaped patches in the traditional "Flower Garden" quilts (Fig. 4-5, and C in the color section) are only 2 inches across, but by increasing the size of the patches to 6 inches across, you can make a contemporary version with less sewing involved.

The easiest way to decide upon the overall design of your quilt is to make sketches of your ideas with colored pencils. Experiment with different color combinations—even a simple design can be visually exciting if made in vibrant colors. Try various ways of setting the pattern blocks together and experiment with borders of different proportions. The quilt, "Geometry 101" (F in the color section), is a simplified version of the traditional "Fan" pattern that was enlarged by borders in the two colors used for the appliqué design. If you are making a contemporary version of the "Flower Garden" quilt, consider adding a straight-edge border, which not only serves to enlarge the quilt with a minimum of sewing but eliminates the problem of finishing off the scalloped edges. Keep in mind that some patterns, for instance, the crazy quilt, can be set together in a variety of ways —as an overall design, or as block units set together in a stripped or latticework effect. On the other hand, patterns such as the "Log Cabin" (Fig. 5-4) or the "Orange Peel" (Fig. 4-32) are effective only when the unit blocks are set together to create an overall design.

Designing your own pieced pattern is fun and easy, too. Cut squares out of paper, divide some of them into equilateral triangles, and put the squares and triangles together in various combinations. You can come up with a tremendous variety of designs by using a three-color scheme, but don't forget that the geometric pieces of the design must fit into the square block units like the pieces of a jigsaw puzzle.

Beware, however, of using curved shapes in making your own pieced pattern. The two contemporary pieced quilts pictured in F in the color section are based on a design that employs the sine curve. On paper, the pattern appears to be simple enough, but when the fabric pieces are sewn together on the wrong side, the curves run in opposite directions and it is necessary to stretch the fabric to make the curves fit together as smoothly as possible. Be sure to experiment with sewing the pattern together before you cut out all the fabric pieces for an entire quilt, and discover that the pattern is difficult to piece.

Drafting the pattern and estimating fabric needed

After you have decided upon the overall design of your quilt, make a full-size drawing of the pattern for the individual block unit. All the quilt patterns shown make finished quilt blocks of 12 inches square, and can be enlarged by using graph paper. Then, make a drawing of each piece of the pattern on cardboard, using carbon paper to

FIG. 8–1.

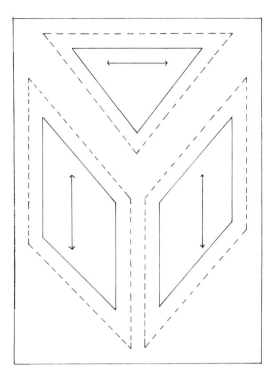

transfer from the master drawing. *Be sure to add ¼ inch for seam allowance onto the dimensions of each piece of the pattern* (Fig. 8-1). Cut out the cardboard pieces with sharp scissors; they are the templates for marking the pattern on the fabric. If the templates become frayed from use, make new ones so that all the pieces for the entire quilt are cut accurately.

To estimate how much fabric you will need, separate the pieces of the cardboard pattern by the colors that you intend to use for the block pattern. Most of the fabrics suitable for making a quilt come 36 inches wide. Measure the pieces of one color in a block unit and estimate how many times they will fit into a width of 36 inches. If, for example, there are four red pieces in each block unit, and sixteen red pieces will fit into a piece of fabric 1 yard square, the pieces for four block units can be cut from 1 square yard of red fabric. Determine from the drawing of the overall design of your quilt how many block units make up the design, and divide the total by the number of block units obtained from 1 square yard of fabric. Repeat this procedure for each color that will be used in the individual block unit.

Don't forget to estimate the fabric needed for borders or for plain blocks between the pattern blocks, if these are part of the overall design, and for the backing of the quilt. Be generous in your estimates of the fabric needed. It is better to end up with a little more fabric than you actually need, rather than not having enough to finish your quilt.

Choosing the fabric

The time and effort you will put into making your quilt certainly demand that you invest in good-quality fabric. Cotton is the most practical fabric for a quilt intended for functional use because it is sturdy and washable. Silks, satins, and velvets are suitable only for a decorative quilt, such as the Victorian crazy quilts, which will require dry cleaning. Lightweight woolens and corduroys also can be used to make heavier quilts and comforters, but the same kind of fabric should be used throughout the quilt. Combining silk pieces with cottons or woolens will shorten the lifetime of the quilt, for the fragile silk will wear out more quickly. The only exception would be in making a decorative wall hanging where a variety of fabrics could be combined to add textural contrast as part of the design.

The new synthetic fabrics, particularly the knits, are not suitable for quiltmaking because they stretch and fray easily. A quilt made with synthetic fabrics will not lay smoothly or wear well. A small percentage of synthetic fibers, at the most 30 percent, combined with cotton, contributes to the washability of the fabric, but any higher percentage of synthetic fibers weakens the fabric. It's a good idea to examine the manufacturer's specifications of the contents of any fabric before purchasing it.

Also, when buying washable fabric, be sure to check that it is preshrunk and colorfast. Always wash all fabric in very hot water before using it, and in particular, test the colorfastness of red, which bleeds easily if the dyeing was poor. Dipping fabric in boiling water with a small amount of vinegar added may help to set the color, but it is better not to use questionable fabric at all than to have the color run during later washings.

Choose fabrics that are sturdy but soft. "Tissue"-quality fabrics will be difficult to work with, as will be fabrics that are stiff because they have been treated with a dressing. Test the quality by grasping the fabric in both hands and tugging gently; if it holds its shape but is soft to the touch, it will be suitable for making a quilt. Cotton velvets are easier to work with than the slippery rayon velvets. Silks and satins should be firmly woven.

Be sure to buy all the fabric needed for your quilt at the same time. It is difficult to match colors unless the fabric comes from the same bolt, and to find the same print later is a matter of sheer luck. To be on the safe side, cut out all the pieces for your quilt pattern as soon as you purchase the fabric, so you will know for certain that you have all the fabric needed.

Traditional quiltmakers usually use unbleached muslin or sheeting for the backing of their quilts because these fabrics are sturdy and are made wider than ordinary cottons. However, I prefer to make my quilt backing in the predominant color of the design on the quilt top, so that the quilt can be used on either side. Depending on the quilt design, you might even want to use a contrasting print for the quilt backing.

Cutting the fabric

Accuracy in cutting the fabric is the crux of quiltmaking. If all the pieces of the pattern are not cut exactly, it will be a hopeless task to try to fit the pattern together. Also, careful placement of the templates on the fabric saves wasting and possibly running out of fabric before all the pieces are cut.

Press the fabric smooth, and lay it flat on a large working area. Draw a thread to ascertain the straight of the fabric. Place the tem-

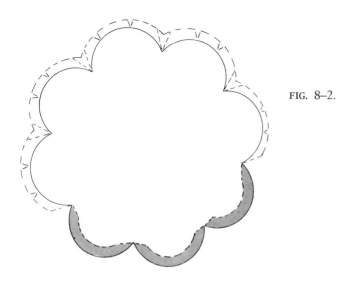

FIG. 8–2.

plate carefully on the wrong side of the fabric, so that the long edge of the pattern runs parallel to the lengthwise threads of the fabric. Diamond shapes and right-angle triangles should have two sides on the straight of the fabric (Fig. 8-1). Allow $\frac{1}{8}$ inch between the placement of pieces of the pattern for space in cutting. Be sure that each piece lies correctly on the straight of the fabric, and that stripes or prints run in the same direction.

Mark around the edge of the template with a pencil on light-colored fabric, and with dressmaker's chalk on dark-colored fabric. Cut out the pieces carefully with sharp scissors, and separate the pieces according to shape and color. Keep all of one kind together by stringing them on a thread or by storing them in separate envelopes.

For appliqué pieces, turn under the $\frac{1}{4}$-inch seam allowance of each piece and crease the turned edge with your fingers. On rounded edges and sharp corners, make a small notch about $\frac{1}{8}$ inch in the seam allowance to keep the edge of the piece smooth (Fig. 8-2). Traditional quiltmakers prefer to baste the edges of the appliqué pieces in place, using a long, loose stitch with the knot of the thread on top of the piece so the basting stitches can easily be pulled out later. However, it is faster to simply press the edges of the appliqué pieces with a steam iron and a damp cloth, using a template to make a sharp, smooth edge.

To cut the bias strips that frequently are used in appliqué designs, draw diagonal lines, 1 or 1½ inches apart, on the fabric and cut along the lines. Turn the edges of the strips under and press in place.

Sewing a pieced quilt {Fig. 8-3}

Hold the patches firmly with right sides together. Unless the fabric is dark-colored, white thread usually is used for sewing pieced quilts because it is stronger. Taking short, even stitches, sew along the ¼-inch seam allowance, ending a row of stitches with several back-stitches to secure it. The ¼-inch seam allowance must be maintained throughout the quilt, and until your eye becomes accustomed to measuring it automatically, mark the seam allowance with pencil on each patch.

As you finish sewing each seam, crease it to one side of the patch with your thumb. Trim the excess seam allowance to avoid bunching. When you have finished piecing all the block units, and *before* you set them together, press all the seams to one side. The seams of a pieced quilt should never be pressed open as that weakens the construction of the quilt. To straighten the edges of the block unit into a perfect square, "block" it by pulling the edges straight with your fingers and pinning the corners to the ironing board. Then cover the block unit with a damp cloth and steam-press from the edges into the center of the block.

Compare each block unit, as you finish it, with the previous ones to make sure they all are the same size and fit together exactly. By checking your work as it progresses, you can easily correct any errors before you reach the stage of assembling the block units together.

When all the block units are completed, lay them out in the over-all design and pin them together to ensure that they are perfectly aligned. Traditional quiltmakers frown on anything but hand-sewing in making a quilt, but sewing the block units together by sewing machine makes the construction of the quilt more sturdy, and it's

FIG. 8–3. Piecing a "Nine-Patch"
pattern.

faster, too. After the block units are set together, press the quilt top
again to make sure that all the seams are flat and the surface of the
quilt lies smoothly. If the quilt top is puckered before you begin the
quilting, the finished quilt will never lie smoothly.

Sewing an appliqué quilt

Assemble the overall design, or the design of all the block units,
before you begin sewing, so that the design will be accurate. Lay the
larger pieces of the design on the background fabric and pin them
in place; then fit the smaller pieces in place by tucking their edges
under those of the larger pieces.

Begin by sewing down the smaller pieces of the design, using tiny
hemming stitches so that the longer part of the stitch is on the wrong
side and the edge of the appliqué piece is barely caught by the stitch.

Use thread the same color as the individual pieces of the design. Embroidery stitches, such as the buttonhole, the featherstitch, the herringbone, or the cross-stitch, can be used to emphasize details of the design.

It's easy to create a relief effect in an appliqué design by stuffing parts of the design with synthetic fiberfill batting. Cut a piece of batting the same shape but slightly smaller in size than the appliqué piece, and place the batting under the appliqué piece before stitching it down.

To appliqué with your sewing machine, follow the guidelines given in the instruction manual for your particular machine. After the appliqué work is completed, either by hand-sewing or machine, block the background fabric and press it on the wrong side, protecting the appliquéd work with a terry towel to keep it from flattening.

Sewing a crazy quilt

There are two methods of making a crazy quilt. The second, although more time-consuming, ensures that the crazy quilt will be the desired shape and size when finished.

Using the first method, cut the fabric scraps into a variety of shapes —squares, rectangles, triangles, and curved pieces—and fit the shapes together on a large working surface (Fig. 8-4). Experiment with different combinations of adjoining shapes and colors to make a handsome design, cutting the pieces when necessary to fit them together. Overlap the pieces by $1/2$ inch and turn in the raw edges of the top piece. Baste the pieces together and then stitch over the seams with decorative embroidery stitches to hold the pieces in place. Featherstitching was a popular embroidery stitch used on crazy quilts of the Victorian era, but any of the embroidery stitches, or a combination, can be used. Embroidery floss should be in colors that complement the colors of adjoining patches.

The second method utilizes unbleached muslin for a backing, cut

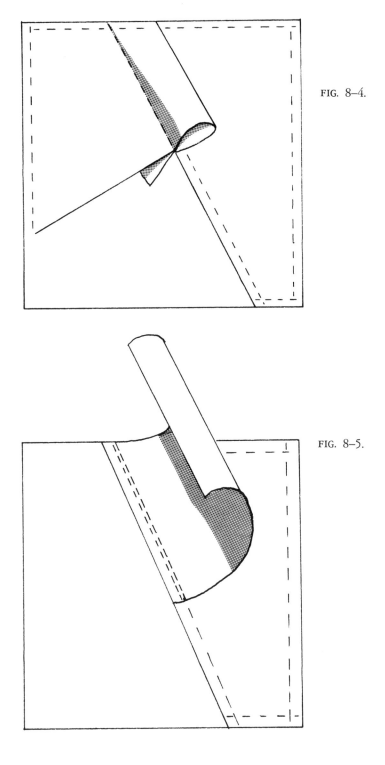

FIG. 8–4.

FIG. 8–5.

to the desired size either for an overall crazy-quilt design or one that is made in individual block units. To begin, place a fabric scrap that has a right angle in the upper corner of the backing, and baste the top and right-angle side of the patch to the backing. Select a second patch that has a straight edge on the top and a side edge that fits with the free edge of the first patch. Place the second patch face down on the first, and sew the free side of the patches together, using a $\frac{1}{2}$-inch seam allowance. Turn the second patch face out and baste the top edge in place on the backing (Fig. 8-5). Continue assembling the patches on the backing in this way, until the backing is completely covered. Take care that each patch is laid back smoothly and tacked in place so that the backing is not stretched out of shape. After the crazy quilt has been assembled, embroidery stitches can be used to decorate the seams.

The crazy quilt requires no filler but does need a lining. Although it is not quilted, the top should be tacked to the lining with decorative stitches in the centers of some of the patches, evenly spaced across the quilt.

Sewing a puffed quilt

The puffed or "biscuit" quilt is another decorative design that is not quilted. The technique of making a puffed quilt is very simple—each puff is made by sewing a silk or velvet square to a muslin square and then stuffing the puff with batting. The puffs or biscuits are sewn together to make any size quilt desired.

Begin by cutting 3-inch squares from silk or velvet, and $2\frac{1}{4}$-inch squares from muslin. With the wrong sides facing, pin the silk or velvet square to the muslin square at the corners. On three sides of the square, pleat the extra silk or velvet and pin into place on the muslin. Stuff the puff with batting through the open side, then pleat the open side and pin into place. Baste around the four sides, close to the edge. Sew the puffs together in rows with right sides facing, using a $\frac{1}{4}$-inch seam allowance. Press the seams open. Line the quilt top and secure the lining by tacking in evenly spaced positions on the quilt back. Tack through the lining, catching the seam allowance under the puffs so that the tacking does not show on the puffed top.

Quilting

Quilting may be done by hand—using either the traditional quilting frame or an embroidery hoop—or by sewing machine, which will be discussed in a later section.

To prepare the quilt top for quilting, the pattern is marked on the top before it is joined with the batting and the backing. Carefully select a quilting pattern that complements the overall design of your quilt. You can buy perforated quilting patterns, or you can make your own patterns out of cardboard, utilizing the designs shown or your own creations. Perforated patterns are used by laying the pattern on the quilt top with the rough side down and rubbing powder or colored chalk through the perforations. Cardboard patterns are used by marking around the patterns with dressmaker's chalk or faint pencil marks. The chalk is easily brushed off once the quilting is finished, and the pencil marks, although less desirable, will not be too noticeable if you are careful to quilt on top of the marks. Straight-line "plain" quilting patterns can be marked on the quilt top by using a ruler and chalk or pencil.

After the quilting design has been marked on the quilt top, assemble the three layers of the quilt, using the floor as your working space so the layers can be spread out smoothly. Put down the backing with its wrong side up, and on top of that lay the batting. Be sure that you have purchased sheet batting, either the cotton batting with a glazed surface or the synthetic fiberfill batting. Batting comes in standard sizes for single and double beds, but if you are making a larger quilt you will have to piece on an additional length by joining together the pieces of batting using doubled thread in wide,

FIG. 8–6.

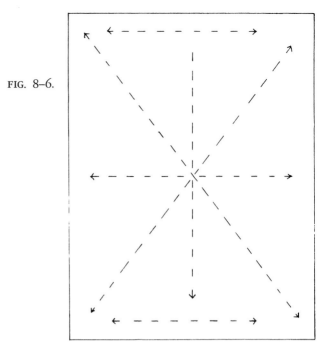

overlapping cross-stitching. Never try to stretch the batting to fit your quilt—it will only tear.

Smooth out the batting on top of the backing fabric, making sure that there are no wrinkles. Traditional quiltmakers baste the batting in place and then baste again when the quilt top is in place, but it is possible to baste all three layers together at one time if you work carefully. Place the quilt top right side up on top of the batting and pin the three layers together. Then baste diagonally across the quilt in two directions, and across the length and width of the quilt, and finally across both ends and down both sides (Fig. 8-6). Later, when the quilting is finished, the edges of the quilt are bound with bias binding, or the top edge is turned under the bottom edge and hemmed down.

Another way to finish off the quilt is to lay the quilt top right side down, then place the backing right side down on top of it with the batting as the top layer, and baste the three layers together. Machine-stitch around three sides of the quilt, catching all three layers with the stitches. Then turn the quilt inside out so that the three layers are in the proper order. When you finish quilting, the fourth and open edge of the quilt is turned under the bottom edge and hemmed down. Although it is rather awkward turning the quilt inside out, the advantage to this method is that the batting is firmly held in the seams of the quilt, which is particularly important when quilting with a hoop.

The traditional quilting frame consists of two long parallel bars the width of the quilt with two shorter parallel bars at right angles to form a rectangle. For a quilting bee, a larger frame, the size of a double-bed quilt, is used so that the quilt can be spread out full-length and at least ten women can quilt at one time (Fig. 3-1). However, for an individual quilter, the long parallel bars are placed no more than two arm-lengths apart. The quilt is attached to the frame by securely sewing the top and backing layers to strips of heavy material that are tacked on the long parallel bars. The top and bottom ends of the quilt are attached to the bars and are rolled up so the quilting begins in the middle of the quilt. The quilter starts working midway in the exposed area of the quilt and sews toward herself. When she finishes one side, she works on the other until the entire area is quilted and the bars then are rolled over to expose another unquilted area.

The frame is supported by legs at the four corners, or rests on the backs of four chairs if they are the right height. It is important that the frame be at a height so the quilter can comfortably sit with her legs under the frame and her arms outstretched to reach over the quilt. The height of the chair in which the quilter sits also should be considered in adjusting the height of the quilting frame.

You can easily make a quilting frame by purchasing two bars of wood, each $1\frac{5}{8}$ inches by $1\frac{5}{8}$ inches and 9 feet long, and two shorter bars of the same dimensions but only 4 feet long. Make sure the bars have no rough spots that might snag the quilt fabric by sanding and covering them with a coat or two of shellac. Nail heavy material such as cotton tape or ticking on the two long bars in such a way that the nail heads will be covered by the material when the ends of the quilt are rolled on the bars. Overlap the four corners of the frame and secure them with C-clamps (Fig. 3-1). Two sawhorses provide adequate support for the quilting frame but should be adjusted to a comfortable height.

If you prefer to use a hoop instead of a quilting frame, you can purchase a standard quilting hoop on a stand or use a large-size embroidery hoop. When quilting with a hoop, the quilting also begins in the center of the quilt and proceeds toward the edges. Pull the quilt taut in the hoop and smooth excess fullness toward the edges of the hoop. As the quilting nears the edges of the quilt, use a smaller embroidery hoop to hold the layers of the quilt taut.

To quilt, use a short, sharp needle—No. 8 or No. 9—and strong white thread—No. 40 or 50. The hand that does not hold the needle is placed underneath the quilt to guide the stitching. The quilting stitch is a short, even running stitch and there are two ways to make it. One way is to first push the needle down through the three layers of the quilt and then, in a separate motion, push it up again close to the first stitch. The second way is to take one or two little running stitches before pulling the needle through. The stitches should be of equal length on both sides of the quilt. Experiment to find out which method is easier for you by quilting a small piece of fabric on an embroidery hoop so you can easily turn the work over to examine the stitches on the underside.

To begin quilting, make a knot at the end of the thread and pull the knot into the batting layer of the quilt so it doesn't show. To end, make a backstitch and run the thread through the batting layer before cutting it off.

Take care to prevent your fingers from becoming sore by using tape on the finger that pushes the needle and on the fingers of the hand that guides the quilting stitch.

After the quilting is finished, remove the quilt from the frame or hoop and trim the edges evenly on all four sides, removing any batting that is sticking out. Bind off the quilt edges in one of two ways, either by folding the top edge of the quilt under the bottom and hemming it in place, or by binding the edges with bias strips. Lay the bias binding, right side down, on the top edges of the quilt, and sew through the binding and all three layers of the quilt, using a $1/4$-inch seam allowance. Fold the binding under the bottom edge of the quilt and hem down. You will need to use bias binding if your quilt has scalloped edges.

Quilting by sewing machine

It's easy to quilt individual block units on a sewing machine. Baste the three layers of the block unit together, leaving the edges open. Carefully mark the quilting pattern on all the block units before beginning the quilting. Make sure that the overall quilting pattern will align correctly when the blocks are set together.

The best patterns to use are "plain" quilting done on the diagonal with a straight stitch. These can be done with or without a special quilting foot attachment, but curved-line patterns require the use of the quilting foot so the pattern can be followed accurately. Set the stitch length control between six and twelve per inch, and adjust the pressure to slightly heavier than mediumweight fabrics. Experiment on scraps before beginning the actual quilting to determine the proper stitch length and pressure for the fabrics you are using.

Starting in the middle, quilt outward to within $\frac{3}{16}$ inch of each edge of the block. Follow the pattern diagonally to one corner, do the same for the other three corners, then fill in the pattern between. Be careful not to pull the quilt block through the machine. If the quilting stitches are uneven or puckered, the stitch length and pressure are not properly adjusted.

When all the quilting is finished, set the block units together by seaming the quilt top on the wrong side. Check that the quilting pattern is aligned as you put the blocks together. Then loosely baste together the batting, and finish the quilt by blind-stitching the seams on the backing side.

It is possible to quilt a crib-size quilt on a sewing machine but a larger quilt is too bulky to handle easily, and the quilting stitches are apt to be uneven. Baste the three layers of the quilt together and mark the quilting pattern on the top. Pull half of the quilt under the foot of the sewing machine and roll it tightly. Beginning in the center, quilt outward to the edge that has been rolled under the foot of the machine. When all the quilting on that half of the quilt is finished, start at the center, with the unquilted part rolled under the foot of the machine, and quilt across the unquilted half. Again, the best patterns to use are "plain" quilting done on the diagonal. "Plain" quilting should be done first and "fancy" patterns filled in later.

Quilted wearing apparel

A quilted evening skirt, quilted velvet lapels on a man's smoking jacket, or a quilted robe are only a few of the many garments that you can easily make with machine-quilting. Select an uncomplicated garment pattern without tucks or gathers. Cut two pieces of fabric, one for the outer layer and one for the backing, for each piece of the garment pattern. Be sure to cut each fabric piece slightly larger than the paper pattern as the quilting will cause some shrinkage. Mark the quilting pattern with dressmaker's chalk on the outer pieces of the pattern. Follow the instructions for machine-quilting individual quilt blocks. Depending on the particular garment, you may want to separate the sheet batting into a thinner layer to avoid a bulky appearance when the garment is finished.

To make a handsome tote bag, use heavy fabric such as denim, sailcloth, or mattress ticking for the outside, and plain or printed cotton for the lining. It's fun to create your own pieced or appliquéd design, or you can simply outline-quilt the design of a printed fabric with contrasting colored thread.

Trapunto, or Italian quilting

Since trapunto is a technique for decorative quilting without the use of batting, it can be done on any firmly woven fabric—cotton, linen, silk, satin, or velvet—and shows up best when the fabric is plain-colored. Use a large, simple outline design for trapunto quilting, such as a floral and leaf motif or a scroll design (Fig. 8-7).

Baste the fabric to a loosely woven backing, such as cheesecloth, with the wrong sides together. Draw the design on the backing. Using a running stitch, double-outline-stitch the design $1/8$ inch on either side of the drawn lines. Be careful to stitch evenly as the underside will be the side that shows when the trapunto is finished. Pad the $1/4$-inch trough between the two rows of stitches by drawing yarn or cording through the trough with a blunt yarn needle (Fig. 8-8). Take care not to catch the outer fabric with the needle. If the raised design on the outer fabric does not stand out enough, run a second strand of yarn or cording through the trough. After the design has been padded, attach a lining to conceal the layer of cheesecloth.

Flights of fancy

You can inexpensively add the decorator touch to your home furnishings with a quilted bedspread or even quilted upholstery. Use a heavy cotton with a dramatic print or a printed velvet, and outline-quilt the print in a contrasting color. In making a bedspread, it's easier to first quilt the lengths of fabric, then sew the bedspread together, following the directions for assembling a quilt made of individually quilted block units.

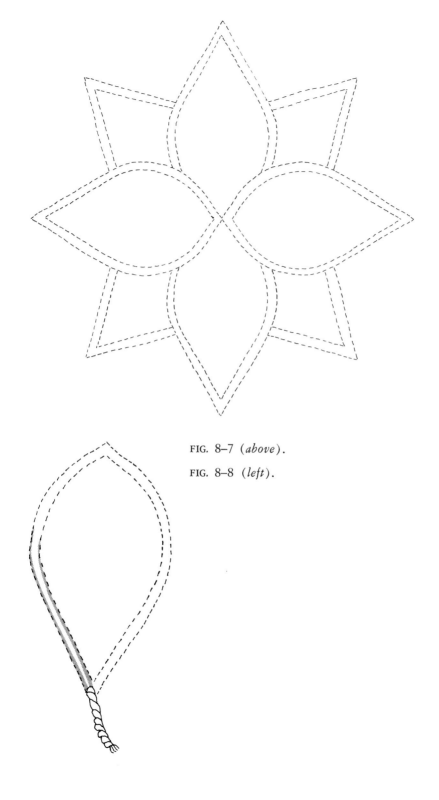

FIG. 8–7 (*above*).

FIG. 8–8 (*left*).

Other decorating ideas are throw pillows with pieced or appliquéd designs, or a patchwork wall hanging, or even a three-dimensional "soft" sculpture. Once you discover for yourself how easy it is to use the techniques of quilting, the possibilities will be as limitless as your imagination.

BIBLIOGRAPHY

ANGLE, PAUL M. (ed.), *Prairie State*, The University of Chicago Press, Chicago, 1968.

BRUSH, DANIEL HARMON, *Growing Up with Southern Illinois*, R. R. Donnelley and Sons Co., Chicago, 1944.

BURLEND, REBECCA AND EDWARD, ed. by Milo Milton Quaife, *A True Picture of Emigration*, Citadel Press, New York, 1968.

COLBY, AVERIL, *Patchwork Quilts*, Charles Scribner's Sons, New York, 1965.

COSCO, ETHEL REESER, *Christian Reeser*, The Story of a Centenarian, privately printed.

FINLEY, RUTH E., *Old Patchwork Quilts and the Women Who Made Them*, J. B. Lippincott Co., Philadelphia, 1929.

HAKE, ELIZABETH, *English Quilting Old and New*, Charles Scribner's Sons, New York, 1937.

HALL, CARRIE A., AND KRETSINGER, ROSE G., *The Romance of the Patchwork Quilt in America*, Caxton Printer, Caldwell, Idaho, 1936.

HALL, ELIZA CALVERT, *A Book of Hand-Woven Coverlets*, Little, Brown, Boston, 1927.

HOSTETLER, JOHN A., *Mennonite Life*, Herald Press, Scottdale, Pennsylvania, 1954.

ICKIS, MARGUERITE, *The Standard Book of Quilt Making*, Dover, New York, 1949.

LANGDON, WILLIAM CHAUNCY, *Everyday Things in American Life, 1776–1876*, Charles Scribner's Sons, New York, 1941.

MCKIM, RUBY SHORT, *One Hundred and One Patchwork Patterns*, Dover, New York, 1962.

PETO, FLORENCE, *American Quilts and Coverlets*, Chanticleer Press, New York, 1949.

———, *Historic Quilts*, American Historical Company, New York, 1939.

ROBERTSON, ELIZABETH WELLS, *American Quilts*, Studio Publications, New York, 1948.

TILLSON, CHRISTIANA HOLMES, *A Woman's Story of Pioneer Illinois*, R. R. Donnelley and Sons, Chicago, 1919.

WEBSTER, MARIE D., *Quilts, Their Story and How to Make Them*, Doubleday, Page and Company, New York, 1926.

INDEX